Cambridge Elements ≡

Elements in Quantitative and Computational Methods for the
Social Sciences
edited by
R. Michael Alvarez
California Institute of Technology
Nathaniel Beck
New York University

UNSUPERVISED MACHINE LEARNING FOR CLUSTERING IN POLITICAL AND SOCIAL RESEARCH

Philip D. Waggoner
University of Chicago

CAMBRIDGE
UNIVERSITY PRESS

CAMBRIDGE
UNIVERSITY PRESS

University Printing House, Cambridge CB2 8BS, United Kingdom

One Liberty Plaza, 20th Floor, New York, NY 10006, USA

477 Williamstown Road, Port Melbourne, VIC 3207, Australia

314–321, 3rd Floor, Plot 3, Splendor Forum, Jasola District Centre, New Delhi – 110025, India

79 Anson Road, #06–04/06, Singapore 079906

Cambridge University Press is part of the University of Cambridge.

It furthers the University's mission by disseminating knowledge in the pursuit of education, learning, and research at the highest international levels of excellence.

www.cambridge.org
Information on this title: www.cambridge.org/9781108793384
DOI: 10.1017/9781108883955

© Philip D. Waggoner 2020

First published 2020

A catalogue record for this publication is available from the British Library.

ISBN 978-1-108-79338-4 Paperback
ISSN 2398-4023 (online)
ISSN 2514-3794 (print)

Additional resources for this publication at www.cambridge.org/waggoner

Unsupervised Machine Learning for Clustering in Political and Social Research

Elements in Quantitative and Computational Methods for the Social Sciences

DOI: 10.1017/9781108883955
First published online: December 2020

Philip D. Waggoner
University of Chicago
Author for correspondence: Philip D. Waggoner, pdwaggoner@uchicago.edu

Abstract: In the age of data-driven problem-solving, the ability to apply cutting edge computational tools for explaining substantive phenomena in a digestible way to a wide audience is an increasingly valuable skill. Such skills are no less important in political and social research. Yet, application of quantitative methods often assumes an understanding of the data, structure, patterns, and concepts that directly influence the broader research program. It is often the case that researchers may not be entirely aware of the precise structure and nature of their data or what to expect of their data when approaching analysis. Further, in teaching social science research methods, it is often overlooked that the process of exploring data is a key stage in applied research, which precedes predictive modeling and hypothesis testing. These tasks, though, require knowledge of appropriate methods for exploring and understanding data in the service of discerning patterns, which contribute to development of theories and testable expectations. This Element seeks to fill this gap by offering researchers and instructors an introduction clustering, which is a prominent class of unsupervised machine learning for exploring, mining, and understanding data. I detail several widely used clustering techniques, and pair each with R code and real data to facilitate interaction with the concepts. Three unsupervised clustering algorithms are introduced: agglomerative hierarchical clustering, k-means clustering, and Gaussian mixture models. I conclude by offering a high-level look at three advanced methods: fuzzy C-means, DBSCAN, and partitioning around medoids clustering. The goal is to bring applied researchers into the world of unsupervised machine learning, both theoretically as well as practically. All code examples will leverage the cloud computing platform Code Ocean to guide readers through implementation of these algorithms.

Keywords: clustering, unsupervised machine learning, computational social science, R

Isbns: 9781108793384 (PB), 9781108883955 (OC)
Issns: 2398-4023 (online), 2514-3794 (print)

Contents

1   Introduction   1

2   Setting the Stage for Clustering   7

3   Agglomerative Hierarchical Clustering   13

4   K-means Clustering   25

5   Gaussian Mixture Models   34

6   Advanced Methods   42

7   Conclusion   56

     References   58

1 Introduction

When people think of machine learning, visions of complex neural networks, support vector machines, or random decision forests tend to come to mind. While these are indeed common machine learning methods, there is another widely used, but distinct class of machine learning: clustering. Clustering, which is more aptly situated in *unsupervised* machine learning, allows researchers to explore, learn, and summarize large amounts of data in an efficient way. Before diving into clustering and its application in political and social research, consider first the distinction between supervised and unsupervised machine learning to better appreciate precisely how clustering works and why it is a valuable approach to exploratory data analysis (EDA), and political and social research more specifically.

Two key components are central to unsupervised machine learning. First, in unsupervised learning, the researcher works with unlabeled data, meaning classes are not predetermined or specified, and thus there is no expected outcome to be predicted or to predict some other outcome. Yet, in a broad research program, researchers can and often do use unsupervised learning techniques, such as clustering, to label data (also called feature extraction in machine learning research), and then feed this output to a supervised classifer, for example. But on its own, unsupervised machine learning works almost exclusively with unlabeled data. This relates to the second key component, which is that unsupervised learning precludes any meaningful engagement by the researcher *during* the modeling process. This is in comparison to *supervised* learning, where model parameters are tuned and training data are set by the researcher, often for predictive purposes. With such preprocessed data and a clear outcome in mind, model fit and output are relatively easily diagnosed and inspected. As such, in the unsupervised learning world, there is no outcome or dependent variable being predicted nor are there parameters to be tuned to result in stronger statistical models used for inference. Rather, the researcher feeds unlabeled data to a learning algorithm and allows patterns to emerge, typically based on similarity among observations (within-group homogeneity) and dissimilarity between groupings of observations (between-group heterogeneity). Such an endeavor is especially valuable in EDA, where a researcher is interested in both recovering underlying, nonrandom structure in data or feature space, while also simplifying and summarizing large amounts of data in an intuitive, digestible way, but with minimal assumptions or interference with the algorithm.

Though there is a trade-off between *exploration* (unsupervised) and *confirmation* (supervised), it is important to note that each are valuable in their respective spheres, and can even strengthen each other (Tukey, 1980).

When a researcher is concerned with fitting a model to data to minimize some prediction error rate or build a maximally accurate learner, supervised techniques may be more appropriate. Yet, when that researcher is more concerned with exploring and summarizing data, perhaps as a step in the broader research program, then unsupervised techniques may be preferred. Indeed, in unsupervised machine learning, the patterns that emerge are meant to be simplifications of more complex, underlying patterns that naturally exist in the data. Whether these patterns accurately reflect "real life" or preconceptions of substantive phenomena is often left to the researcher to decide. In addition to the validation techniques discussed later in the Element, there are additional ways to verify and validate results of unsupervised learners, such as comparison across multiple and different algorithms or often domain expertise. Thus, the idea here is that emergent patterns should be evaluated on the basis of domain expertise, as well as checked against other methods and algorithms, as any researcher would do in more common "robustness checks." While this Element stays away from normative prescriptions for which approach to data exploration and analysis is "better" (as better so often does not exist), the goal at present is to introduce a new, *additional* way of thinking about, exploring, and understanding patterns in data.

The focus of this Element, then, is on clustering, which is one of the most common forms of unsupervised machine learning. Clustering algorithms vary widely and are exceedingly valuable for making sense of often large, unwieldy, unlabeled, and unstructured data by detecting and mapping degrees of similarity between objects in some feature space. Though a key device in simplifying the complexity of data to reveal underlying structure, selecting and fitting clustering algorithms can be complicated for a couple reasons. First, in clustering there is typically no single "right" or "one-size-fits-all" algorithm for a question or problem. The selection of an algorithm depends on a variety of factors such as the size and structure of the data, the goals of the researcher, the level of domain expertise, the transformation of the data, how observations are treated, and so on. As such, clustering is often a process of selecting, fitting, evaluating, repeating, and then comparing across different specifications of a single algorithm or between multiple algorithms using the same data. This process will become much clearer as the Element progresses.

Next, and related, consider performance evaluation. In regression, for example, researchers are often interested in how well the model fit and whether it performed as expected (e.g., did learner X sufficiently minimize the prediction error rate compared to learner Y?). But recall, in unsupervised learning there are no parameters to be estimated nor are there clear expectations for emergent patterns as there are in supervised learning. As a result, evaluation of unsupervised algorithmic performance is rarely straightforward. To go about this, which is unpacked at length throughout this Element, the researcher should always compare across several specifications and algorithms, as well as apply domain expertise related to the problem and data in question. Such a holistic approach to data analysis should be characteristic of all research programs, whether supervised or unsupervised.

For example, suppose a researcher is interested in exploring and learning about American voting behavior. The researcher, armed with a large, unlabeled dataset of election returns may begin with hierarchical clustering to see whether groupings exist among voters in the country. Using visual output like a dendrogram (which is discussed later at greater length), may reveal that two broad camps of voters tend to be clustered together. As a starting place, the researcher may suspect these two clusters of voters represent the two major choices of American national elections: Republicans and Democrats. Regardless of the quality of the assumption, the researcher may still be unsure of precisely how and why these clusters among American voters exists. The researcher may progress to specify a more advanced algorithm requiring a little more information, such as the CLARA (clustering large applications) algorithm, assuming two groups exist based on the hierarchical dendrogram from the first stage. If the results corroborate similar patterns revealing two broad groups, then the researcher has a better sense that the data may indeed represent some consequential groupings among the voting population, which could be political parties. However, if there are less clearly defined clusters from the CLARA iteration when two clusters were assumed (based on the first hierarchical clustering stage), then the researcher may want to update the algorithm to hunt for three or four clusters instead of two. In addition to visual corroboration, the researcher can then leverage across common methods of internal validation such as the Dunn index, average silhouette width, or connectivity (all of which are discussed more later) across the different clustering algorithms to understand whether these algorithms and iterations are pointing to similar groupings in the American voting population.

Note that this example began with no clear expectations of patterns that should emerge against which a researcher could compare some *estimated* output to some *expected* output (as would be the case in *supervised* learning). Rather, the researcher simply fed unlabeled voting data to several algorithms, and observed (and then compared) the emergent patterns. The rinsing and repeating associated with unsupervised learning is central to understanding precisely how unsupervised learning can be effectively leveraged to *learn* about and explore data in a principled manner. Then, once the researcher has learned the data structure and patterns, the remainder of the research program can be adjusted to develop testable expectations, estimate relationships, and generate inferences. In approaching clustering, there should be heavy emphasis on the *learning* part. The researcher begins with some base level interest in the topic and is armed with a rich, yet unlabeled dataset. Prior to making specific predictions, given the lack of clearly defined expectations of how the data are structured, the researcher could specify and compare a number of different algorithms to "let the data speak" freely. Note that these goals of exploring dimensionality and reducing spatial complexity are also present in other methods more commonly employed in the social sciences such as latent variable modeling, multidimensional scaling, and correspondence analysis. Though similar in goals, however, as will be discussed throughout this Element, unsupervised machine learning approaches problems of complexity and dimension reduction from a fundamentally different place. For example, often no effort is made during the modeling process to infer any meaning or definition of the emergent clusters; rather the goal is most often pure discovery. Inference should happen at a different stage. This and other distinctions are frequently revisited throughout the Element.

In order to effectively introduce unfamiliar readers to unsupervised machine learning, it makes most sense to start with the most commonly leveraged form of unsupervised learning: clustering. Within clustering, there are many approaches, as well as even more algorithms *within* these approaches, with many more currently being developed each year to deal with new and unique problems and patterns in data (e.g., mean shifting clustering). As no single work could ever effectively cover all clustering approaches and algorithms, let alone the entirety of unsupervised learning, I begin with and detail the three mostly widely used (and taught) clustering algorithms: first, agglomerative hierarchical clustering; second, k-means clustering ("hard" partitioning); and third, Gaussian mixture models (model-based "soft" partitioning). And for readers interested in going beyond these three approaches, I conclude with a section detailing more complex and recent advances in clustering, though at a higher level: fuzzy C-means clustering; density-based clustering (the DBSCAN algorithm); and partitioning around medoids clustering (i.e., "k-medoids" via the PAM algorithm).[1]

---

[1] Readers should note that the approach to clustering presented in this Element is situated within an unsupervised learning framework, where we are interested in exploring and partitioning unlabeled data. This is distinct from model-based clustering, which estimates parameters and forms clusters in a probabilistic fashion. Though a model-based technique (Gaussian mixtures models) is covered later in this Element for introductory purposes, readers interested in a more technical treatment of model-based clustering should consider the recent book by Bouveyron et al. (2019).

1.1 Running Example: State Legislative Professionalism

I use state legislative professionalism as a running example throughout this Element. I chose this as the example for several reasons. First, and substantively, precisely how to conceptualize and measure the level of professionalism of a state legislative chamber is an ongoing debate. Though originally defined as a static index, which is updated every decade or so (e.g., Squire [1992, 2000, 2007, 2017]), recent advances leveraging multidimensional scaling have offered a dynamic measure (Bowen and Greene, 2014). Regardless of the measurement approach, several inputs discussed below are central to this unique concept, which leads to the second reason for selecting state legislative professionalism as the example. That is, this is a multidimensional concept, the definition of which is continuing to evolve. Third and finally, there is no agreed-upon dimensionality that *should* characterize state legislative professionalism (e.g., two, three, and so on dimensions). So while we will leverage four unique inputs, there is no expected pattern to emerge, consistent with unsupervised machine learning. Rather, natural clusters of state legislatures may exist as a function of these raw inputs alone. This makes the learning component of clustering all the more applicable for my introductory purposes.

The state legislative professionalism data include 950 observations (states) from 1974 to 2010, where each row is a state/year dyad (e.g., "Alabama, 1984"). There are four key inputs of interest: *total session length* (including special sessions), *regular session length* (excluding special sessions), *salaries of legislators*, and *expenditures per legislator*. Total session length ranges from 36 days to 549.54 days. Regular session length ranges from 36 days to 521.85 days. Salaries of legislators are measured in 2010 dollar, and range from 0 (for voluntary legislatures) to $254.94.[2] And finally, expenditures per legislator are measured in thousands of 2010 dollars ranging from $40.14 to $5,523.10. Regarding expenditures per legislators, Bowen and Greene (2014) noted in the codebook that these values "were created by subtracting the total amount paid in salary (number of state legislators × salary or per diem × session length) and then divided by the number of state legislators." The expectation in collecting, and now using, these raw inputs is that they should capture the relative levels of state legislative professionalism. In sum, these data include rich nuance from states with large budgets and well-paid legislators to states with volunteer legislatures and small budgets, making them valuable for such an exercise in unsupervised clustering.

---

[2] Bowen and Greene (2014) note that salaries are "annual salary and/or per diem salary multiplied by length of regular session."

1.2 Visualization as a Key Tool

Whenever possible, I will present visual depictions of algorithmic output in lieu of numeric output, as data visualization can be understood as perhaps the simplest form of unsupervised learning. By plotting data distributions, valuable descriptions on a variety of dimensions are possible. This, as with unsupervised learning more broadly, should lead to a greater understanding of underlying structures in data. The hope, then, is to contribute to a more thorough, better-informed analysis downstream. Also, visualization is a simple, streamlined way to communicate far more than numbers or words alone. For example, from Anscombe's quartet, we know that *exclusive* focus on numeric evaluation can lead to misleading conclusions about data and patterns if we neglect the visual component as well (Anscombe, 1973). This was reiterated in the recent update to Anscombe's quartet, where not four, but 13 wildly different distributions emerged from nearly identical numerical definitions of data (Matejka and Fitzmaurice, 2017). From a star and bull's-eye to a dinosaurus and "X," these distributions, all with the same numerical descriptions down to three decimal places in some cases, point to the need for and value of visualizing data. Therefore, whenever possible, I offer visual tools and depictions of algorithmic output along with discussion to clearly identify and explain the techniques in the most intuitive light possible. The result is a road map for researchers interested in applying these methods in their own research.

1.3 A Word on Programming in R

All examples and code used throughout are executed in the R programming language. Each code chunk will be integrated with *Code Ocean* to allow for direct engagement with and further exploration of all concepts covered in this Element.

Given the use of R, at least a baseline understanding of R and object-oriented programming is expected. Several tools from the Tidyverse will also be used. For users interested in learning more about R as well as the Tidyverse, I recommend starting with Hadley Wickham and Garret Grolemund's book, *R for Data Science* (Wickham and Grolemund, 2016).

Many other tutorials and resources are available online for those interested in learning more about functions, packages, and tasks covered in this Element. Readers are encouraged to fill any gaps in their understanding accordingly, as no tutorial on "getting started with the basics of R" is provided in this Element. Still, every effort is made to clearly explain the presented code chunks and convention both in-text as well as via comments in the code.

The following packages will be used throughout this Element. Readers are encouraged to install all packages first, and then load the libraries using the following code.

```
# first install the packages
install.packages(c("tidyverse", "factoextra", "skimr", "ape",
    "clValid", "cluster", "gridExtra", "mixtools"))

# next, load the libraries
library(tidyverse)
library(factoextra)
library(skimr)
library(ape)
library(clValid)
library(cluster)
library(gridExtra)
library(mixtools)
```

2 Setting the Stage for Clustering

Clustering can be thought of in two main ways, which are dependent on how the data are treated: subdivide the data or not. Subdividing the data means to partition the data into smaller clusters. Partitioning methods are discussed more in later sections. The opposite of partitioning or subdividing the data is to cluster data in a pairwise fashion. This can take shape in one of two ways: recursively from the top down (divisive hierarchical clustering) or from the bottom up (agglomerative hierarchical clustering). Hierarchical clustering is addressed as the first algorithm in this Element in the following section.

Prior to fitting clustering algorithms, we must first set the stage. This typically consists of assessing clusterability and then defining distance (similarity and dissimilarity between observations). In this section, we will cover assessing clusterability in two prominent ways (sparse sampling and ordered dissimilarity images), and then discuss widely used methods of calculating distance (Manhattan, Euclidean, and Pearson), the choice of which will strongly influence the clustering output.

2.1 Assessing Clusterability

Recall that unsupervised learning is focused on exploratory data mining where nonrandom data patterns and structures are able to be uncovered. In this vein, an important first step in hierarchical clustering (or any clustering method for that matter) is assessing whether the data are "clusterable." In so doing, we are interested in understanding whether any inherent, underlying clusters exist in the data and thus could be found by any clustering algorithm.

Though there are several methods for assessing clusterability, we will cover two prominent methods: sparse sampling to calulate the Hopkins statistic and ordered dissimilarity images (or "visual assessment of tendency" [VAT] plots) (Bezdek and Hathaway, 2002). ODIs are more widely accepted in the machine learning community, though both are reasonable approaches to assessing clusterability. Combining the results from the Hopkins statistic and the VAT, we will lay a solid foundation upon which we can progress with fitting our agglomerative hierarchical clustering algorithm to learn about the structure of state legislative professionalism.

2.1.1 Sparse Sampling: The Hopkins Statistic

We begin with the Hopkins statistic (H), which uses sparse sampling to measure spatial randomness between observations. The H statistic calculates the probability that some given data is generated by a uniform (random noise, with no clusters) distribution or not (nonrandom, with clustering likely). In this technique, we are creating a random, synthetic version of the original data set, which is called the sampling window. We then compare this data to the original data to see whether these data sets produce similar distributions, where we are interested in whether the original data is random (no clusters), compared to the synthetic data set, which we *know* is random. We start by setting up a null hypothesis test:

H_0: the data is uniformly ("equally") distributed
H_A: the data is not uniformly distributed

Under this hypothesis testing framework, the goal is to determine whether distances between real points significantly differ from distances between the randomly generated points, all pointing to whether clusters are likely to exist in the actual data or not. In brief, we start by uniformly sampling n observations, p_i, from our **actual** data, D. Then, for each observation $p_i \in D$, we find its nearest neighbor, $p_i\prime$. We calculate the distance between p_i and $p_i\prime$ and denote it as $u_j = dist(p_i, p_i\prime)$. Next, we create a **synthetic** (simulated) dataset, $D\prime$, drawn from a random, uniform distribution with n observations (q_i), with the same standard deviation as D. Here again, for each observation $q_i \in D\prime$, we want to find its nearest neighbor $q_i\prime$, and then calculate the distance between q_i and $q_i\prime$ and let $w_j = dist(q_i, q_i\prime)$ denote this distance (Kassambara, 2017). Using these data, we now calculate H, which is the mean distance between observations in the actual data divided by the sum of the mean distances across the actual *and* simulated data,

$$H = \frac{\sum_{j=1}^{m} u_j^d}{\sum_{j=1}^{m} u_j^d + \sum_{j=1}^{m} w_j^d} \tag{2.1}$$

Regarding interpretation, while there is a lack of consensus in the literature on a "rule of thumb" value denoting ideal clusterability, values closer to 1 suggest that natural clusters are likely to exist in the data, leading to rejection of H_0.

Before calculating the statistic, we need to first load and organize the data a bit. We also need to standardize the data by setting all input features on a common scale, with $\mu = 0$ and $\sigma = 1$. To do so, we will leverage several tools from the Tidyverse (Wickham and Grolemund, 2016), and then, to calculate the H statistic, we will leverage the `factoextra` package (Kassambara, 2017).

```
# First, filter by 09/10 session
st <- x %>%
        filter(sessid == "2009/10") %>%
        select(-c(fips, stateabv, sessid,
                  mds1, mds2, year)) %>%
        na.omit(st); skim(st)

states <- st$state # will need this later

st_scale <- data.frame(scale(st[,2:5]))
rownames(st_scale) <- states

# Hopkins Statistic
h <- get_clust_tendency(st_scale, nrow(st_scale)-1)
h$hopkins_stat
```

With the data loaded and cleaned, the next bit of code is used to calculate the H statistic using the `get_clust_tendency` function from the `factoextra` package, which we can ultimately store in object h to allow for quicker access for future use. This function returns two main objects of interest: the H statistic, and the ordered dissimilarity object, which is the next clustering assessment test.

Running the code returns the H statistic of 0.172. Recall that we are looking for higher H values, and 0.172 seems low to indicate clustering. Though this may be the case, this underscores the value of multiple tests discussed and reiterated throughout this Element. As such, in the next subsection, we turn to the other main test to assess clusterability, which is the ordered dissimilarity image.

2.1.2 Ordered Dissimilarity Images

Recall the admonishment from Anscombe's quartet, where relying only on numeric evaluation of results can result in a limited and possibly skewed version of the story. Thus, given the lower H statistic of 0.172, I now transition to a second method, which is to visualize clustering tendency using an ordered dissimilarity image.

Ordered dissimilarity images (ODI) are visual depictions of the range of dissimilarity between observations. Higher values mean greater dissimilarity between observations. Generating ODIs requires two steps: first, visualize the dissimilarity matrix, and second, order the objects based on spatial similarity, where objects of greatest similarity are placed close to each other, and distant from those less similar. The result is a large blocking-type image, where colors are valuable to aid in interpretability.

Regarding interpretation, then, the ODI will reveal large blocks if clusters exist. If no underlying clusters exist, then there would be no large blocks in the ODI, revealing an image of many tiny points randomly distributed with no systematic blocking pattern, pointing to a lack of relationship in the underlying dissimilarity across observations. Such patterns are effectively visual depictions of the sparse sampling procedure described earlier. In sum, in the ODI we are looking for large, systematic blocking patterns revealing clusterability. No large blocks suggests low to no clusterability.

To ease interpretation, I specify the colors in the code to be associated with degrees of dissimilarity via the gradient() argument. Updating our previous code, I set low dissimilarity (or high similarity) to be black, and high dissimilarity (or low similarity) to be red. The midrange is set to gray. If there is an underlying clusterability in our state legislative professionalism data, then we would expect to see large blocks in the ODI.

```
h <- get_clust_tendency(st_scale, # data set
            nrow(st_scale) - 1,
            gradient = list(low = "black",
            mid = "gray",
            high = "red"))

(h_plot <- h$plot + labs(fill = "Range of\nDissimilarity"))
```

In Figure 2.1, we can see one large block in the lower left of the ODI, and a smaller block in the upper right of the ODI. This suggests that there is likely one large cluster and one small cluster in the data. Paired with the relatively small H statistic, this suggests that there are likely clusters that naturally exist in the state legislative professionalism data, but perhaps less obvious than we might have expected. The best way to gain clarity on these clusters, then, is

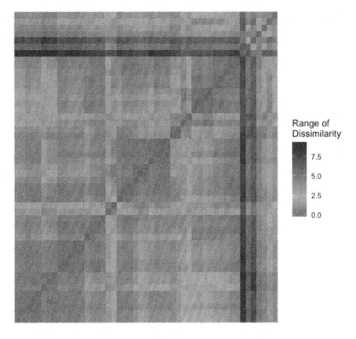

Range of Dissimilarity

7.5

5.0

2.5

0.0

Figure 2.1 Ordered Dissimilarity Image

to proceed with the clustering algorithms in light of the patterns observed in Figure 2.1.

2.2 Measuring Distance

Upon standardizing (scaling) the input features as we previously did, the next important step in setting the stage for clustering is determining an appropriate measure of distance. Recall, we are interested in uncovering patterns in data. Patterns inherently suggest some notion of similarity. We can think of similarity (and thus dissimilarity) in a variety of ways such as density, location, and even correlation. The way distance is measured will impact on the clustering results, so checking across certain distance measures is never a bad idea. And though I offer some general guidance on various distance measures, there is no firm rule for which measure is best, as different applications require different measures. Here again, domain expertise and multiple measures are an excellent approach to ensuring high-quality research and design.

In this subsection, we will cover the three most widely used measures of distance for quantitative input features: Manhattan ("city block" or "Minkowski") distance, Euclidean distance, and Pearson (correlation) distance. To be sure, there are many other distance measures such as Eisen cosine distance, Gower's distance for mixed data, and so on. Though there is insufficient space to cover these in this Element, readers are encouraged to look more into distance measures that fit the needs of a given project.

2.2.1 Manhattan Distance

First, we consider Manhattan distance, which is sometimes referred to as "city block" distance or, erroneously, the Minkowski distance measure. The reason for this is that the Manhattan and Euclidean distance measures are generalizations of the Minkowski measure. Readers should note that all of these distance measures can be easily "vectorized" (e.g., $||d_m||$) to efficiently account for multidimensional spaces. For clarity of presentation, we start with the base Minkowski form for observations p and q,

$$d_m(p, q) = \left(\sum_{i=1}^{n} |p_i - q_i|^m \right)^{\frac{1}{m}} \tag{2.2}$$

where m is the distance order between points p and q, across all observations, i. Setting $m \geq 1$ defines some true distance, $d(p, q)$. So, setting $m = 1$, we get the Manhattan distance measure between points p and q,

$$d_{manhattan}(p, q) = \sum_{i=1}^{n} |p_i - q_i| . \tag{2.3}$$

The Manhattan measure is also sometimes referred to as the L_1 distance measure, as we are setting $m = 1$. Note that the Canberra distance measure is simply a weighted version of the Manhattan distance, $d_{canberra}(p, q) = \sum_{i=1}^{n} \frac{|p_i - q_i|}{|p_i| + |q_i|}$.

2.2.2 Euclidean Distance

As we are building on the Minkowski measure, setting $m = 2$ gives us the L_2 distance measure, or the classical Euclidean distance measure. Arguably the most widely used distance measure in clustering applications, the Euclidean captures the distance between observations p and q by taking the square root of the squared, pairwise distances,

$$d_{euclidean}(p, q) = \sqrt{\sum_{i=1}^{n} (p_i - q_i)^2}. \tag{2.4}$$

Or, equivalently, to see the similarity to the Minkowski measure, we could write Equation (2.4) as

$$d_{euclidean}(p, q) = (\sum_{i=1}^{n} (p_i - q_i)^2)^{\frac{1}{2}}. \tag{2.5}$$

Interestingly, Euclidean distance is sometimes referred to as "as-the-crow-flies" distance, as we are using the Pythagorean theorm to actually calculate the distance.

2.2.3 Pearson Distance

Finally, another widely used measure, though based on correlation, is Pearson's correlation measure. This measure captures the distance between points p and q based on how closely they correlate, rather than how close they are in space, implying observations could be spatially far from each other, but highly correlated. This would result in a different clustering configuration than the previously addressed L_1 and L_2 spatial measures. It is calculated

$$d_{pearson}(p, q) = 1 - \frac{\sum_{i=1}^{n}(p_i - \bar{p})(q_i - \bar{q})}{\sqrt{\sum_{i=1}^{n}(p_i - \bar{p})^2 \sum_{i=1}^{n}(q_i - \bar{q})^2}}. \qquad (2.6)$$

Regardless of the selected measure, the output will be a dissimilarity (similarity) matrix, where high values suggest high dissimilarity (similarity), and low values suggest low dissimilarity (similarity).

3 Agglomerative Hierarchical Clustering

Starting with hierarchical clustering is valuable when introducing readers to clustering, as this method is especially useful when fully formed expectations on patterns and data structures do *not* exist. Essentially assumption-free (i.e., not specifying the number of clusters to search for a priori as in k-means clustering, discussed more next), hierarchical clustering measures the connectivity between observations in some feature space, or dataset. By employing connectivity between observations and then distance between clusters, we can use the output from the clustering algorithm to visualize their spatial similarity to each other at a variety of levels, typically in the form of a dendrogram, which is a tree-like structure showing progressively nuanced similarities between observations. Hierarchical clustering, then, can inform subsequent clustering methods based on revealed patterns. For example, if the dendrogram reveals two natural groupings, or clusters, then a second stage may initialize a k-means algorithm with two clusters. Upon specifying the k-means algorithm, the researcher would then be able to directly compare the internal validity of both clustering algorithms to determine which is best at clustering the data along a variety of dimensions (e.g., connectivity, compactness). There are two types of hierarchical clustering: agglomerative (bottom-up) and divisive (top-down).

Agglomerative hierarchical clustering iterates from the bottom up, and begins by treating each observation as its own cluster (or "singleton"). Then, in pairwise fashion, singletons are joined with other singletons based on some linkage method, which is discussed more in a moment. Then, as clusters grow, they are connected with other clusters, and this process iterates until all clusters are joined in a single large cluster including all singletons. Divisive clustering is the inverse of agglomerative, starting with all observations in a single cluster, and recursively iterates until each observation is a singleton. Though both techniques have their value in different applications, agglomerative hierarchical clustering is far more frequently used, especially in the social sciences. Thus, in this section we will focus on applying and learning agglomerative hierarchical clustering.

3.1 Linkage Methods

Hierarchical clustering algorithms are unique in that they require specifying a linkage method, in addition to determining the distance measure, the latter of which all clustering algorithms must do first. Thus, with our standardized distance data, we can fit a hierarchical clustering algorithm, but as the algorithm proceeds in a pairwise fashion, we need to specify precisely how these pairs are joined together. The linkage method is the mechanism for determining this.

Similar to the distance measure, there are many linkage methods from which to choose. Here, we will cover four of the most commonly used: complete, single, average, and Ward's linkage.

Complete linkage links clusters based on the maximum distance between two clusters, such that the outermost points of given clusters determine the linkage. Inversely, upon calculating all pairwise distances, single linkage uses the minimum distance (dissimilarity) between two clusters to determine linkage. Average linkage, then, joins clusters based on the mean cluster dissimilarity. Finally, Ward's linkage method joins clusters based on combinations that result in the smallest increase in the sum of squared errors, calculated across all clusters.

For the applications in this section, we will fit hierarchical clustering algorithms using all four of these linkage methods to compare configurations and how the configurations are intimately tied to the selected linkage method. Here again, it is useful to point out that, like distance measures, there is no guidance in the literature on which linkage method is best. Selection of linkage method is usually dependent on domain-specific preferences (e.g., centroid linkage is popular among geneticists). It is recommended that researchers follow a similar pattern to the one shown in this Element and compare across several linkage methods to uncover natural patterns as efficiently as possible.

It is important to reiterate that only hierarchical algorithms require specification of a linkage method, yet all clustering algorithms require specifying and calulating a distance between observations. The distance measure determines how similarity and dissimilarity are defined in feature space, while the linkage method determines how singletons, which turn into bigger clusters, are joined together. Both linkage and distance measures are required for hierarchical clustering, while only distance measures are required for all other clustering techniques.

3.2 Fitting a Hierarchical Clustering Algorithm

To this point, we have standardized the state legislative professionalism data, assessed the clusterability using the Hopkins statistic and the ODI, detailed widely used distance measures and computed our dissimilarity matrix, and also detailed the four most common linkage methods for the agglomerative hierarchical clustering algorithm. With the stage set, we are now able to fit the algorithm across each of the four linkage methods and then compare the output to explore and understand the professionalism of state legislatures.

To fit the clustering algorithm, we will directly create the dissimilarity matrix using the Euclidean (L_2) distance measure, as it is most common in social science applications. To change the distance measure, researchers should simply specify the preferred distance measure by updating the method argument in the dist() function call (e.g., dist(x, method = "manhattan")). Next, we will use the hclust() function in base R and change the linkage method by passing each method (e.g., "average", "complete") to the method() argument. Note that it is relatively uncommon (and largely useless) to evaluate the numeric output of a hierarchical clustering algorithm. As such, we will produce the results visually via a dendrogram using the second function, fviz_dend(), from the factoextra package. Recall that dendrograms are tree-like structures that place observations on different "branches" based on similarity, which in our case is spatial. The Y axis of the dendrogram reflects the distance between the observations, where large branches suggest clearer clusters, and thus greater dissimilarity between other clusters. The following code produces the output shown in Figure 3.1.

```
# First, generate the distance matrix of Euclidean distances
st_scale_dist <- st_scale %>%
        dist(); head(st_scale_dist) # inspect the first 5 obs

# Now, fit and visualize
hc_single <- hclust(st_scale_dist,
            method = "single")
```

```
single <- fviz_dend(hc_single, cex = 0.65, k = 2,
            color_labels_by_k = FALSE, rect = TRUE,
            main = "")

hc_complete <- hclust(st_scale_dist,
            method = "single")
complete <- fviz_dend(hc_complete, cex = 0.65, k = 2,
            color_labels_by_k = FALSE, rect = TRUE,
            main = "")

hc_average <- hclust(st_scale_dist,
            method = "single")
average <- fviz_dend(hc_average, cex = 0.65, k = 2,
            color_labels_by_k = FALSE, rect = TRUE,
            main = "")

hc_ward <- hclust(st_scale_dist,
            method = "ward.D2")
ward <- fviz_dend(hc_ward, cex = 0.65, k = 2,
            color_labels_by_k = FALSE, rect = TRUE,
            main = "")

grid.arrange(single, complete, average, ward,
            nrow = 2, ncol = 2)
```

Running this code produces four dendrograms with boxes indicating trees cut at two clusters, for visual purposes only. These dendrograms, presented in Figure 3.1 reveal interesting clustering patterns. For example, California sticks out as either alone (when linkage is single, complete, and average) or clustered with only a few other states (when linkage is Ward's method), including New York, Illinois, Massachusetts, Pennsylvania, Ohio, and Michigan.

Zooming in a bit, we can inspect the top ten states across each of the four inputs to see if these offer clues as to why the states might be clustered together. To do so, we will leverage a few Tidyverse commands, including the pipe operator and the `arrange()` command.

```
head(st %>% # total session length
    arrange(desc(t_slength)), 10)

head(st %>% # regular session length
    arrange(desc(slength)), 10)

head(st %>% # salary
    arrange(desc(salary_real)), 10)

head(st %>% # expenditures
    arrange(desc(expend)), 10)
```

Running this code produces the descriptive results in Tables 3.1 through 3.4. Any states in the Ward's linkage algorithm are in bold for descriptive purposes. From here we can see that at a minimum, four of the seven states

Table 3.1 Top Ten States: Total Session Length

State	Total Session Length (Days)
New York	458.15
California	390.00
Massachusetts	385.02
Arizona	286.13
Ohio	258.00
Pennsylvania	242.00
Michigan	213.00
Colorado	205.20
North Carolina	181.76
South Carolina	169.53

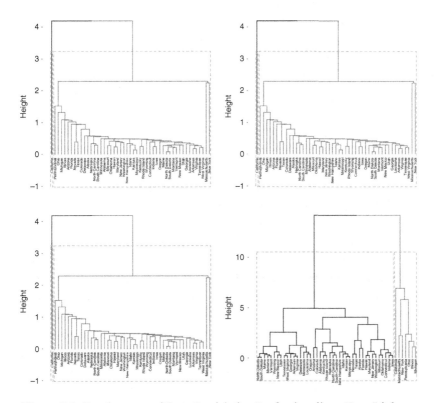

Figure 3.1 Dendrogram of State Legislative Professionalism: Four Linkage Methods

Table 3.2 Top Ten States: Regular Session Length

State	Regular Session Length (Days)
New York	427.15
Massachusetts	385.02
California	270.00
Ohio	258.00
Michigan	213.00
Pennsylvania	211.00
Colorado	205.20
Arizona	197.38
North Carolina	181.76
South Carolina	169.53

Table 3.3 Top Ten States: Legislator Salaries

State	Salary
California	213.41
Michigan	160.61
New York	160.30
Pennsylvania	157.91
Illinois	136.78
Ohio	122.16
Massachusetts	117.43
Hawaii	98.21
New Jersey	96.50
Maryland	87.71

from the algorithms fit with Ward's linkage method appear in the top ten states (in expenditures), and at a maximum all seven states are in the top ten states (in salaries). And because California is at the top of most input features, include nearly double the second most in expenditures and salaries, we are starting to get the sense that California is perhaps the most professionalized of the state legislatures, and also that salary seems to play a big part in determining spatial similarity, at least when we specify Ward's linkage method.

Another, but similar view of dendrograms is called a cladogram (or "triangular" dendrogram), presented in Figure 3.2. Cladograms are useful in that they offer a slightly cleaner look at the clustering patterns but reveal the same

Table 3.4 Top Ten States:
Expenditures per Legislator

State	Expenditures
California	5523.10
Pennsylvania	2434.62
Florida	2087.29
New York	2027.92
Texas	1551.93
Alaska	1493.84
Nevada	1281.94
New Jersey	1178.87
Michigan	1143.00
Washington	991.26

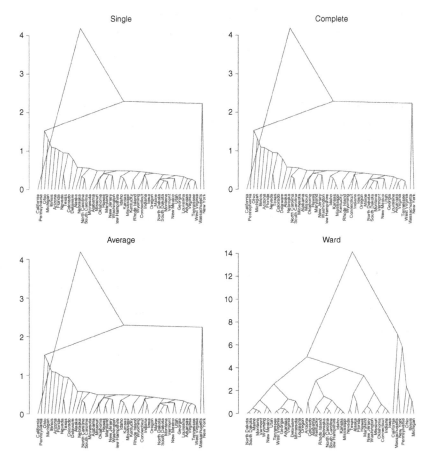

Figure 3.2 Cladograms of State Legislative Professionalism: Four Linkage
Methods

information, with the Y axis as the measure of distance, and longer branches reflecting unique clusters. Here again, we see that California is by itself in three of the four linkage methods. This suggests that perhaps, based on the four input features of salary, expenditures, total session length, and regular session length, California is in its own league, so to speak. We will get a clearer sense of these patterns, as well as the relationship of California's legislature to other state legislatures, as we progress in the Element with the other clustering techniques.

Regardless of the conclusions drawn from the patterns presented in Figures 3.1 and 3.2, as well as descriptively in Tables 3.1 through 3.4, as noted in the introduction, unsupervised clustering is all about summarizing and reducing the complexity of data. And though general patterns seem to be emerging (e.g., relatively few "professional" state legislatures compared to many that may be "less professional"), it is important to reiterate that clustering does *not* estimate relationships of interest. Rather, the question emerging from these patterns is the aforementioned "parsimony" (unsupervised) and "perfection" (supervised) trade-off, whereas in clustering we are interested in parsimony rather than "perfection" associated with model tuning or parameter fitting. As researchers are using these methods to make data increasingly understandable, researchers must also take great care in interpreting patterns, as well as how those interpretations are incorporated in the broader research program. A good starting place in "taking great care" is validation of the algorithm's performance across numerous specifications (covered in the following subsection), along with comparing cluster configurations *and* validation statistics across several clustering approaches (covered throughout the remainder of this Element).

3.3 Internal Algorithmic Validation

As we are working with unlabeled data in unsupervised learning, and *not* outcome prediction, it is important to underscore the relatively limited options for determining "optimality" when it comes to cluster configurations and algorithmic output. As such, it is also important to preface this subsection on internal validation by noting that optimality of algorithm and cluster selection is not deterministic, meaning that there is no single diagnostic test or measure that definitively supports the selection of one algorithm or specification over many others that exist. In the previous iterations of our clustering algorithm in Figures 3.1 and 3.2, all we could conclude was that as the number of groups, k, increased, so too did the precision of the clusters in our data. Recall, in clustering we are interested in a useful simplification of the data. In an effort to validate the algorithms as effectively as possible, then, we must rely on internal measures of validation, where we are interested in an algorithm's *internal* performance, measured by comparing numerous specifications of a single algorithm.

Internal validation consists of evaluating the quality, performance, and results of the algorithm across numerous specifications (e.g., dendrogram tree cutting). Similar to our earlier discussion on assessing clusterability, the clustering patterns we have uncovered thus far are valuable only insofar as they mirror the underlying and nonrandom structures in the data as closely as possible. In other words, in clustering, and unsupervised machine learning more broadly, we are interested only in applying these techniques if they get us closer to understanding substantive patterns in the real world; this is especially true in social and political research. Validating an algorithm's performance, then, is an important final step in clustering, whether hierarchical or otherwise.

Though there are many ways to validate performance (e.g., internal, stability, external), I focus on internal validation for a few reasons. First, output from any algorithm is functionally useless if the algorithm did not perform as it should. Yet, precisely defining "as it should" can be tricky, as we will observe later. Second, internal validation can be used to offer an estimate of the likely "optimal" number of clusters, though again, optimality varies dependent on researcher needs, research goals, subsequent specifications, domain expertise, and so on. Finally, and most importantly, evaluating the *quality* of the clusters uncovered by the algorithm is vastly important, as we infer many things about patterns, trends, and behavior based on the clusters that emerge from the algorithm.

For internal validation measures, it is common practice to rely on *comparison* of algorithmic results to an index, of which there are dozens (e.g., Hartigan index, Calinski-Harabasz index, C index). As opposed to external validation approaches, where clustering results are compared to a priori known clusters (i.e., *supervised* clustering), internal validation measures rely on assessing the algorithmic results based on known properties in the data (Brock et al., 2011). Thus, similar to interpreting the Hopkins statistic, though no "rule of thumb" values are typically suggested for interpreting these indices, the goal is to compare values across both indices as well as various specifications (e.g., comparing multiple index values across configurations for $k \in \{1, 2, \ldots, K\}$). This internal validation process will become clearer as we progress through the next exercise. Here, we will cover three widely used internal validation metrics: connectivity, the Dunn Index, and average silhouette width.

The first measure is connectivity, which assesses the spatial placement of observations in a given cluster, relative to other observations in that same cluster. Connectivity ranges from $0 \rightarrow \infty$, where lower values mean a better cluster, as connectivity seeks to minimize within-cluster variance. The Dunn index and average silhouette width are both "non-linear combinations of the compactness and separation" of observations in a cluster (Brock et al., 2011, 3). The Dunn index ranges from $0 \rightarrow \infty$, where higher values suggest better performance. Similarly, though the silhouette width is within the $[-1, 1]$ interval rather than ranging continuously, it too should be maximized, suggesting better clustering, relative to other possible configurations. Recall that the main goal of clustering in unsupervised learning is to maximize homogeneity *within* a cluster and heterogeneity *between* clusters. In so doing, the algorithm is locating and defining the shape of the underlying structure in the data. Each of these internal measures captures the extent of this goal by assessing connectivity between observations in a cluster (measure one), density within clusters, and then separation between clusters (measures two and three).

To assess the internal validation of our clustering algorithm using these three measures, we will leverage the clValid() function from the clValid package (Brock et al., 2011). This powerful function allows for simultaneous comparison of multiple clustering algorithms across all three of the internal validation measures. The validation measures are easily plotted using the plot() function in base R. The ability to assess internal validation across multiple clustering algorithms will be valuable in later sections where we will simultaneously evaluate all algorithms explored in this Element. But for now, we will only assess the hierarchical clustering algorithm explored thus far. Running the following code will produce the results for all three measures presented in Table 3.5.

```
# define a distance matrix; inspect first few obs
st_scale_dist_m <- st_scale_dist %>%
        as.matrix(); head(st_scale_dist_m)

# calculate internal validation scores for 2 to 10 clusters
st_prof.internal <- clValid(st_scale_dist_m, 2:10,
                clMethods = c("hierarchical"),
                validation = "internal")
summary(st_prof.internal)
```

We can see in Table 3.5, which displays the values from each test for different specifications of the algorithm for number of clusters ranging from two to ten, that across all internal validation indices, the algorithm with two clusters performs best, as it relates to minimizing connectivity, and maximizing cluster compactness and separation. The optimal scores (for $k = 2$) for connectivity, the Dunn Index, and average silhouette width are 4.98, 0.52, and 0.77, respectively. We can also visualize the internal validation results from

Table 3.5 Internal Validation Scores

				Number of Clusters					
	2	3	4	5	6	7	8	9	10
Internal Index									
Connectivity	4.9774	7.1202	12.1821	14.1821	21.7258	22.2603	24.5103	31.7536	33.9536
Dunn Index	0.5218	0.5218	0.4753	0.4753	0.3589	0.3589	0.3589	0.2046	0.2046
Silhouette Width	0.7724	0.7183	0.5927	0.5828	0.3933	0.3179	0.3105	0.2930	0.2849

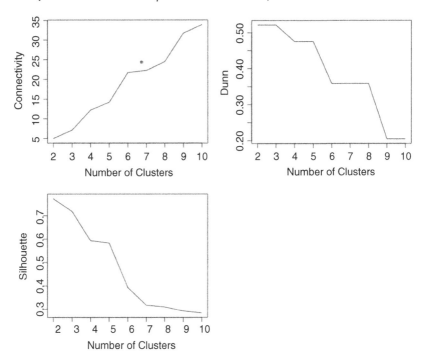

Figure 3.3 Internal Validation of Hierarchical Algorithm

our `clValid` object using the base R `plot()` command. Running the following chunk produces the output shown in Figure 3.3

```
par(mfrow = c(2, 2))
plot(st_prof.internal, legend = FALSE,
     type = "l",
     main = "")
```

The patterns in Figure 3.3 visually corroborate the numeric output in Table 3.5. Across all three tests of internal validation, the most internally valid specification was the algorithm with two clusters, suggesting ultimately that two clusters likely characterize these data well. This is the same pattern seen in the initial dendrogram in Figure 3.1.

It is important to highlight that other performance assessment tests beyond internal tests also exist. A widely used technique is randomization distributions for statistical inference (sometimes called "permutation" tests). The idea behind randomization inference is to simulate data under some statistical assumption or set of assumptions (e.g., assuming uniformity). In such a world, researchers can test whether assumptions hold and thus whether distribution-based expectations are reasonable. These types of tests, though different in scope from internal validation, are useful for other goals such as bridging the gap between unsupervised and supervised learning. For example, researchers may wish to check whether the clusters that emerge from the unsupervised stage inform a supervised task, such as building a learner to classify some set of future unlabeled data points. For an excellent introduction to simulations and randomization-based inference along with helpful R code, see Chapter 10 in Baumer, Kaplan, and Horton (2017).

3.4 Suggestions for Further Reading

- Johnson (1967)
- Friedman, Hastie, and Tibshirani (2001) (Chapter 14)
- Day and Edelsbrunner (1984)
- Gong et al. (2016) (substantive application)

4 K-means Clustering

The next clustering method we explore is k-means clustering. K-means clustering is a relatively simple, iterative unsupervised learning algorithm that is a close relative to hierarchical clustering as we discussed in the previous section. It is often considered in comparison to hierarchical clustering because it, too, is searching for patterns in the data and grouping based on minimizing within cluster variance, while simultaneously maximizing between-cluster variance. The goal is to produce a summarized and simplified look at the data based on natural, nonrandom patterns that inherently exist in the data. However, k-means and hierarchical clustering differ in a fundamental way, and that is in how they treat the data as clusters are searched for. In hierarchical clustering, clusters are formed in a pairwise fashion, whereas in k-means, the data are actually subdivided or partitioned to form mutually exclusive, nonoverlapping clusters.

Another important difference between these clustering approaches is that the number of clusters, *k*, must be set a priori by the researcher in k-means clustering. Though slightly resembling supervised learning, k-means is still considered an unsupervised learner in that there is no outcome being estimated, nor is there any model training or parameter tuning. K-means clustering, rather, follows the same steps as many other unsupervised clustering algorithms, where data are fed to the algorithm with the goal of revealing nonrandom, underlying structure in feature space.

K-means clustering is in the centroid class of clustering algorithms, where minimization of within-cluster variance is computed based on distances between each observation and a centroid in a given cluster. The centroid is most often defined as the mean of the cluster, hence the name "k-*means*." The "k" in this name represents the number of clusters to guide partitioning the feature space, with each cluster centering around a computed cluster mean. Iterating the search many times, the algorithm returns visual and numerical summaries of the uncovered clusters.

Formally,

$$WSS(C_k) = \sum_{x_i \in C_k} (x_i - \mu_k)^2 \tag{4.1}$$

where x_i is the ith observation belonging to cluster C_k, and μ_k is the mean of C_k, defining its centroid. The goal then is to assign observations to clusters, such that the total within the cluster sum of squared Euclidean distances between observations in a given cluster, k, is minimized. Readers should refer back to the subsection on measuring distance for the discussion and formula for calculating Euclidean (L_2) distance. We then seek to minimize the within-cluster sum of squares (*WSS*) for all clusters, C_k,

$$\sum_{k=1}^{k} WSS(C_k) = \sum_{k=1}^{k} \sum_{x_i \in C_k} (x_i - \mu_k)^2. \tag{4.2}$$

4.1 Implementing K-means Clustering in R

As we have assessed the clusterability of our state legislative professionalism data as well as calculated our Euclidean distance matrix in earlier sections, we are ready to implement the k-means clustering algorithm in R on multivariate state legislative professionalism data. To do so in R, we need to first set the seed value, which, given that the k-means iterates in search of the optimal number of clusters based on minimizing within-cluster sum of squares, tells R where to return on subsequent iterations to ensure the same starting values, which aids in reproducibility. This can be any value. Then, we call the kmeans() function in base R to fit the algorithm.[3] The first argument in the data object, which in our case is the scaled state legislative professionalism data, st_scale. The second argument, centers, is the number of prespecified clusters the algorithm should search for, which, given the patterns uncovered in the previous section on hierarchical clustering, we have set at 2. And finally the third argument, nstart, specifies the number of random starts the algorithm should make in clustering the data, which in our case we have set at 25. We will store the fit algorithm in object km.

---

[3] The only required input to fit a k-means algorithm in R is a data object. Distances between obser- vations and the cluster centroids are treated as Euclidean by default when calling the kmeans() function, as this is the most common distance measure. To change the distance measure, users simply need to create a new distance object using the dist() function in base R and specify the desired distance measure in the method argument, and then pass the new distance object to the kmeans() function.

```
# fit the k-means algorithm
set.seed(634)

km <- kmeans(st_scale,
             centers = 2,
             nstart = 25)
```

4.2 Numerically Evaluating K-means

Running the previous code chunk, we now have a fit k-means algorithm to our state legislative professionalism data. In this subsection, we will start with numerically evaluating the output, and then in the following subsection, we will visually evaluate the output.

First, for numerical evaluation, kmeans objects store a lot of useful information. For example, cluster ($cluster) stores the cluster assignment for observation, x_i; centers ($centers) is a centroid measurement, which reflects the distance of each observation, x_i, to the cluster mean for each cluster, C_k; the withinss ($withinss) value stores the sum of squares for each cluster C_k. Further, tot.withinss ($tot.withinss) stores the sum of *all* clusters' sums of squares, which is the sum of the withinss $\forall C_k$. Finally, size ($size) stores the number of observations, x_i, in each cluster, C_k. There are several additional summary statistics stored in kmeans objects, which researchers can access using the str() function, as shown below.

Further, we can view the cluster assignments in table form, with summed values for each cluister, or individually by state with a few lines of code. Run the following chunk to see all of these values and results.

```
# Call structure of the model fit object
str(km)

# Call individual values, e.g.,
km$cluster
km$centers
km$withinss

# Assess/inspect our kmeans object
# Centroids:
table(st_scale$Cluster)

t <- as.table(km$cluster)
t <- data.frame(t)
head(t, 10)
```

Though there is a great amount of useful information presented when running the previous code chunk, a few things stand out. First, when calling the cluster assignments, km$cluster, we see that six of the previous seven states from the hierarchical clustering algorithm with Ward's linkage are again clustered together, including the seeming outlier, California. The only state not clustered with these original seven is Illinois. But interestingly, this information suggests that when we prespecify two clusters and fit a k-means algorithm, six states look quite similar to each other across all four input features, and thus distinct from the other states in the legislative professionalism data set.

For a sample of these assignments in a more intuitive presentation, consider the first ten states and their cluster assignments from the previous code chunk, and presented in Table 4.1. Here again, we can see California as the only state clustered in the second group, out of the first 10 states alphabetically.

Continuing, we can take a closer look at the structure of the algorithm, by calling the str() function from base R. A few important summary statistics are worth highlighting. First, the cluster value, as already discussed, reveals the individual cluster assignments. Second, the centers value is a matrix of individual states' mean distances to the cluster centroids, which are the computed cluster means around which clusters are formed. Further, the total.withinss value is 88.7. As this is the sum of both clusters' within sum of squares, we can check the total based on the two values stored in withinss, which are the within sum of squares for each cluster, where $48.4(C_1) + 40.4(C_2) = 88.8$.[4]

Table 4.1 Ten State Cluster Assignments

State	Cluster Assignment
Alabama	1
Alaska	1
Arizona	1
Arkansas	1
California	2
Colorado	1
Connecticut	1
Delaware	1
Florida	1
Georgia	1

---

[4] Totals slightly vary due to rounding.

4.3 Visually Evaluating K-means

Recall that visualization of trends and clustering is quite valuable, especially in clustering applications. As such, we move now to consider a visual depiction of these cluster assignments. As this is seemingly a multidimensional concept, the clearest way to visualize spatial differences across cluster assignments a scatter plot along raw input values. We will start with looking at states color-coded by cluster assignments, plotted across raw expenditure and salary values. We will then look at color-coded cluster assignments again, but plotted across the other two input features, total and regular session lengths. These plots are side by side in Figure 4.1 following this code chunk. Note that the first couple of lines of code prior to the plots store the cluster assignments by attaching them to the scaled data frame, `st_scale`. This allows for the color coding within the ggplot2 code that follows.

```
st_scale$Cluster <- as.factor(km$cluster) # attach to df
table(st_scale$Cluster)

# First, by expenditures and salaries
ggplot(st_scale, aes(salary_real, expend,
                color = Cluster,
                label = states)) +
        geom_jitter() +
        geom_label(aes(label = states,
                color = Cluster),
                size = 3) +
        xlim(-1.3, 3.7) +
        labs(x = "Salary",
                y = "Expenditures",
title = "State Legislative Professionalism by Expenditures
        & Salary",
subtitle = "Clusters from k-means Algorithm") +
        theme_bw()

# Second, by total and regular session length
ggplot(st_scale, aes(t_slength, slength,
                color = Cluster,
                label = states)) +
        geom_jitter() +
        geom_label(aes(label = states,
                color = Cluster),
                size = 3) +
        xlim(-1.3, 4.5) +
        labs(x = "Total Session Length",
                y = "Regular Session Length",
title = "State Legislative Professionalism by Session Lengths",
subtitle = "Clusters from k-means Algorithm") +
        theme_bw()

# Arrange both side by side
grid.arrange(es, trs, nrow = 1)
```

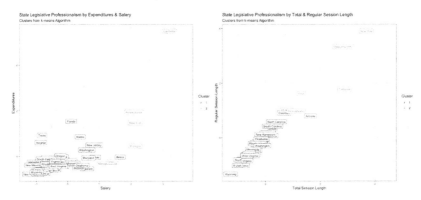

Figure 4.1 State Cluster Assignments across All Input Features

Figure 4.1 displays the visual pattern of cluster assignments by color across all input features in the state legislative data. Several patterns emerge. First, California looks like an outlier when we consider the plot on the left of Figure 4.1 across salary and expenditures. This corroborates the descriptive trends seen in the previous section showing California as having nearly double the budget of the second most state. But interestingly in the right plot in Figure 4.1, we see New York as the outlier when plotting across total and regular session lengths. This suggests that New York has the longest session lengths. Further, we can see the same six states cluster to the upper right of both distributions, though more clearly in the right plot across session lengths. Taken together, based on previous findings on state legislative professionalism (e.g., Bowen and Greene [2014]; Squire [2007]) suggesting that greater professionalism means closer resemblance to the U.S. Congress, in which sessions are quite long and salaries are high, these patterns corroborate this conclusion. Thus, substantively, based on these patterns we would conclude that, conservatively, it would be reasonable to suggest these six states () are "professional," whereas the remaining states are not professional.[5]

4.4 Internal Algorithmic Validation

We now turn to internally validate the k-means algorithmic performance. As previously discussed in the hierarchical validation subsection, any measure

---

[5] Note that in the literature, the classification hierarchy of professionalism sometimes includes a midrange, third category (high, low, volunteer legislatures). But here, allowing the data to "speak freely," as we are interested in doing in unsupervised learning, the natural patterns suggest that two clusters accurately characterize these data. Though this is addressed later on, substantive interpretations are left to the scholars who actively research this topic. This discussion is intended to be illustrative only.

of internal validation is useful only insofar as it provides a picture of the overall quality of an algorithm's performance in comparison to some alternative specification(s), For example, in the k-means case where researchers must prespecify the number of clusters the algorithm should search for, we might be interested in asking the question (via our internal validation metrics), "did the iteration with $k = 2$ minimize within sum of squares more or less than the iteration with $k = 3$, or $k = 4$, or $k = 5$, and so on?"

Here again, we will use the same three, widely used internal validation measures to compare the clustering configurations across numerous alternative specifications, for $k \in \{2, \dots, 10\}$. Further, per the flexibility of the clValid package, we will also compare the k-means iterations to the hierarchical iterations. This will allow for not only *intra*algorithmic comparison, but also *inter*algorithmic comparison. The measures are connectivity, the Dunn Index, and average silhouette width. As a brief refresher, the connectivity measure evaluates the spatial proximity of observations in a cluster, where minimization of within-cluster sums of squares is the goal. The Dunn index as well as the average silhouette width measure the shapes of clusters (within *and* between) as well as the cluster density to gauge cluster compactness and intercluster heterogeneity, where maximum compactness within clusters and maximum heterogeneity between clusters are the twin goals. The following code first generates the numeric validation statistics, and the second chunk of code generates the visual depiction of these results. The numeric output is presented in Table 4.2 and the visual output is presented in Figure 4.2.

```
# First define a matrix (as before with HAC)
st_scale_dist_m <- st_scale_dist %>%
        as.matrix(); head(st_scale_dist_m)

st_prof.internal.k <- clValid(st_scale_dist_m, 2:10,
        clMethods = c("hierarchical", "kmeans"),
        validation = "internal")
summary(st_prof.internal.k)

par(mfrow = c(2, 2))
plot(st_prof.internal.k, legend = FALSE,
        type = "l",
        main = "")
```

Note, first, that the hierarchical clustering internal validation scores remained unchanged, as expected. Thus, when we add k-means to the mix and compare directly, a few points stand out. First, and foremost, across all iterations thus far, two clusters seem to most accurately describe these data. Recall though, that optimality in these terms is strictly *internal*, meaning, based on the minimization or maximization, dependent on the index, the

Table 4.2 Internal Validation Scores: Hierarchical vs. k-Means

			Number of Clusters						
	2	*3*	*4*	*5*	*6*	*7*	*8*	*9*	*10*
Internal Index: Hierarchical									
Connectivity	4.98	7.12	12.18	14.18	21.73	22.26	24.51	31.75	33.95
Dunn Index	0.52	0.52	0.48	0.48	0.36	0.36	0.36	0.20	0.20
Silhouette Width	0.77	0.72	0.59	0.58	0.39	0.32	0.31	0.29	0.28
Internal Index: k-means									
Connectivity	6.82	11.64	13.78	15.78	28.59	31.58	34.29	36.54	40.29
Dunn Index	0.20	0.20	0.37	0.37	0.14	0.14	0.16	0.16	0.18
Silhouette Width	0.75	0.58	0.57	0.55	0.32	0.32	0.33	0.32	0.34

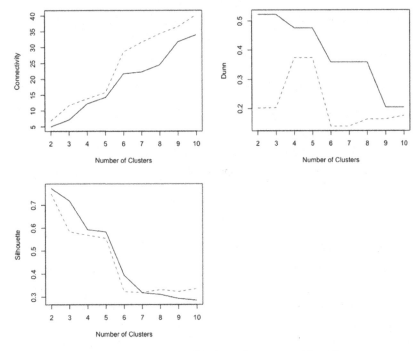

Figure 4.2 Internal Validation of K-means Algorithm

number of clusters with the optimal validation index values is two, suggesting that these algorithms, regardless of their different iterative approaches and approximations, cluster the state legislative professionalism data into two broad groups. And a second and important observation from Table 4.2 is that the hierarchical clustering algorithm outperforms k-means across all validation measures.

Next, we can visualize these results by directly comparing and overlaying each clustering method across all possible clusters from two to 10. Running the second chunk of code above generates this visual comparison in Figure 4.2. The first line specifies a plot pane of 2 rows by 2 columns. The second line leverages the plot command in base R, beginning with the object storing the validation scores from the previous chunk of text, followed by an argument omitting the legend from within the plot pane. The second line specifies a line plot, and the final line omits the plot title. There are many other optional arguments that could be passed to the command, which can be accessed in the package documentation. Consider the plot in Figure 4.2, where the solid black lines correspond with the hierarchical clustering algorithm, and the dashed red lines correspond with the k-means algorithm we just fit, across numerous iterations corresponding with different preset clusters.

Indeed, as discussed above, the hierarchical algorithm outperforms k-means across all measures of internal validation at the optimal cluster level of two.

4.5 Suggestions for Further Reading

- Hartigan and Wong (1979)
- Kanungo et al. (2002)
- Hara et al. (2018) (substantive application)

5 Gaussian Mixture Models

We now come to the final of the three clustering approaches: Gaussian mixture models. In so doing, we transition away from "hard partitioning" (mutually exclusive, nonoverlapping clusters as in k-means) to model-based clustering as a form of "soft partitioning." In soft partitioning, observations could exist in several clusters rather than be assigned strictly to a single cluster. In this section, then, we move to the realm of finite mixture models, which are often used to derive *and* predict clusters in feature space. Mixture models are *probabilistic* models fit to data to derive clusters of observations. The core assumption with this approach to clustering is that there are k mixture components (i.e., "clusters") in some feature space that, together, comprise a mixture or probability distribution, $p(x)$. Though these models can take several forms and can be extended in a variety of ways to account for a variety of needs, from setting cut points in k-modal distributions, imputing missing observations, and even more classic statistical inference, we start here at the base level to offer an intuitive introduction to the concept and a single class of finite mixture models.

In deciding to fit a mixture model for clustering, we are concerned with classification of observations (American states in our case) into components (clusters, as we have thought of to this point). As with the previous examples, we are interested in addressing the following question from an unsupervised machine learning framework: *what, if any, groupings exist in the state legislative professionalism feature space?*

Gaussian mixture models (GMM) are a special, widely used class of finite mixture models, where each component, k, is assumed to be normally distributed. This is an important assumption, because classification of observations in components occurs probabilistically. When we fit Gaussian mixture models to some feature space for classification, then, we are interested in deriving the probability of a given observation, i, being assignedto a component,

k. Formally, the probability distribution, $p(x)$, is comprised of the sum of all normally distributed components, k,

$$p(x) = \sum_{k=1}^{K} \alpha_k \mathcal{N}(x; \mu_k \sigma_k), \qquad (5.1)$$

where α_k is the probability weight, or mixture size, for component k, driving the assignment of observations to components, where $\sum_{k=1}^{K} a_k = 1$. The joint probability distribution, $p(x)$, is defined by the weighted average of all individual components, k. Note that in specifying a GMM, we simply set the parameters assuming a mixture of Gaussians (i.e., in Equation 5.1, $\mathcal{N}(x; \mu_k \sigma_k)$). We could easily set the parameters to assume any distribution, whether binomial, gamma, and so on.

An important consideration with GMM, and thus a deviation from our previous approaches, is the notion of "soft" or "fuzzy" clustering of observations in components. As components are partitioned probabilistically, there is often a degree of overlap between components, where some observations could be assigned to multiple clusters. This is distinct from previous approaches, such as k-means, where we were interested in strictly partitioning the data, allowing for the formation of homogenous clusters based on minimizing distances *within* clusters and *between* observations and the center of the cluster to ensure there is no overlapping between clusters.

Soft clustering assignment of observations based on probabilities could be a useful approach suggesting strong face validity for more complex or ambiguous data sets more closely mirroring reality. However, soft clustering allowing for overlap between components could be a poor representation of real-world observations, especially if the researcher's goal is to form homogenous clusters separated by hard partitions. In the latter case, perhaps a k-means (or the close relative discussed in the following section, k-medoids/PAM) approach would be more ideal. These trade-offs are discussed in the concluding section.

Therefore, in using GMM, which are extensions of k-means clustering, we are fundamentally shifting our conception of both the feature space (i.e., a set of unique, *normally* distributed components) as well as the composition of the components, where similarity between observations assigned to a component is now defined by similarities in the probability of observations being assigned to a given cluster, k, rather than a minimization of some distance metric (e.g., Euclidean distance).

5.1 The Expectation-Maximization (EM) Algorithm

As we are interested in probabilistically deriving components, we are estimating parameters, assuming each component k is normally distributed.

Though more assumptions are imposed on our feature space, GMM are valuable extensions of k-means clustering, in that we can now use both the mean (μ_k) *and* variance (σ_k) to describe the shape of the components, and ultimately reduce the complexity of the feature space, $p(x)$. Though there could be some debate as to whether GMM for clustering are truly unsupervised, this point on feeding data to an algorithm and simply evaluating the output, absent any outcome prediction or parameter tuning, suggests that GMM still belong in the unsupervised learning world, if perhaps a special case.

Though there are several algorithms that can be used to fit the parameters to a data set, the most common by far is the Expectation-Maximization (EM) algorithm. In brief, the EM algorithm is an iterative approach to deriving the probabilistic components in the feature space, where we start by initializing our algorithm to search for k components. We allow each observation to be assigned a probability of belonging to all components, k. Then, ultimate assignment is determined by the greatest probability associated with the kth component.

After initialization, the "E" step consists of randomly selecting a starting place for parameters, but based on the number of components that were set in the initialization step. Then, the relative probability of each observation, i, belonging to all possible components, k, is calculated and ranges between $[0, 1]$. High values suggest the kth component is a good fit for i, and low values suggest the kth component is a poor fit for i.

Then, the "M" step then updates the parameters – μ_k, σ_k, and α_k – for each component, k. Upon convergence, each component, k, is comprised of observations, i, with the highest probability associated with membership to the component, as well as similarity across probabilities for all observations in all components, k. The goal then is to iterate and update the parameters, and build components based on maximizing the probabilistic similarities across each observation for membership in a given component, k.

Convergence occurs and the EM algorithm stops once the fit no longer improves. As maximum likelihood estimation is used to calculate the probabilities for each observation, i, belonging to all components, k, the EM algorithm is iterating the log-likelihood, such that increasing log-likelihood values means a better-fitting model to the data. Convergence, then, suggests the model fit is no longer improving and the parameter estimates are no longer changing substantially, if at all.

5.1.1 Specifying Initial Components

How do we initialize the EM algorithm to fit a GMM? There are several ways to go about this, but the most common and relatively assumption-free is first, fit a k-means algorithm to the same data and base the EM initialization on the clusters that emerge from the k-means contexts; and/or second, visualize the distribution of the data. If multiple distributions could possibly exist, then a safe place to initialize the EM algorithm is based on this visual inspection. For example, if a distribution was bimodal, with two "humps" visually present, then it would be reasonable to initialize the EM algorithm with two components. Or, an alternative approach is randomly initializing the components and then fitting multiple iterations of the model, which allows for comparison and a check on consistency. This is often the preferred approach when virtually nothing is known about the data or domain, which is quite rare in most political and social research contexts.

5.2 Implementing GMM Using the EM Algorithm in R

With the intuition introduced, we can now proceed to an applied case by fitting a GMM to our state legislative professionalism data via the EM algorithm. We first need to initialize the algorithm by setting the components. Suppose we opted to initialize by fitting a k-means algorithm. As we have already done this in the previous section, we will initialize components here to be two, and then inspect additional iterations later in the validation subsection below. Note here we also need to set the seed to allow for reproducibility. Then, we will use the mvnormalmixEM() function from the mixtools package (Benaglia et al., 2009). Note that the "mv" portion of the function is in reference to the multivariate nature of the input features, which in our case is four: total session length, regular session length, expenditures per legislator, and salaries.

```
# set the seed
set.seed(634)

# fit the model
gmm1 <- mvnormalmixEM(st_scale[ ,1:4])
```

Note that upon running the code, the output console shows how many iterations it took for the model to converge. Though each time this code is run the iterations will be different, as the EM is an iterative probabilistic algorithm, the output should be substantively similar. The output from our gmm1 model will include a variety of useful information, such as probability weights for assignments to each cluster, as well as individual quantities of interest associated with each component like the means (gmm1$mu) and standard deviations (gmm1$sigma). Though valuable, a simpler and more informative approach is to visualize the output. To do so, we need to munge the data just a bit to get everything into new objects for plotting. First, store component probabilities in a new data object, posterior_df, and then create a new dichotomous variable, Component, which is the cluster/component assignment, for component probabilities greater than 0.5. Then, we will reattach our state names (previously pulled out and stored in earlier sections) to both our posterior_df object, as well as our original scaled data object, st_scale. Then, storing the cluster assignments from the k-means output for comparison to the posterior_df object, we merge the original scaled data with the posterior data to ease plotting. And the two rename() lines are simply renaming the salary and expenditure variables as these were altered during the merging ("x" was appended to the names). Now, we have a new data frame, full, from which we will plot the output. We start with the GMM output only in Figure 5.1, and then compare to the k-means output in Figure 5.2.

```
# get counts for each component and a little munging
posterior_df <- as.data.frame(cbind(gmm1$x, gmm1$posterior))
posterior_df$Component <- as.factor(ifelse(posterior_df$comp.
                                    1 > 0.5, 1, 2))
posterior_df$State <- states
st_scale$State <- states
posterior_df$Cluster_km <- st_scale$Cluster

full <- merge(posterior_df, st_scale, by = c("State")) %>%
        rename(salary = salary_real.x) %>%
        rename(expenditures = expend.x)

full %>%
        ggplot(aes(salary, expenditures,
                color = Component,
                label = states)) +
        geom_jitter() +
        geom_label(aes(label = states,
                color = Component),
                size = 3) +
        xlim(-1.3, 3.7) +
        labs(x = "Salary",
                y = "Expenditures",
        title = "State Legislative Professionalism by Expenditures &
                Salary",
        subtitle = "Clusters from Gaussian Mixture Model") +
        theme_bw()
```

Most strikingly, the GMM assigns many more states to the second cluster with the original six, including New Jersey, Alaska, Florida, Arizona, Texas, and Nevada. These additional states have mostly higher expenditures than the remaining states. However, they have lower salaries than the original six states. This suggests that the probabilistic assignment takes expenditures more into account than the strict k-means approach or the hierarchical algorithm with Ward's linkage method, both of which seemed to be heavily influenced by total session length and salaries. For a more direct comparison, consider Figure 5.2.

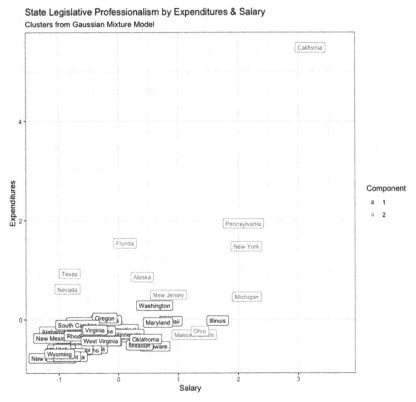

Figure 5.1 Gaussian Mixture Model Output across Salary and Expenditures

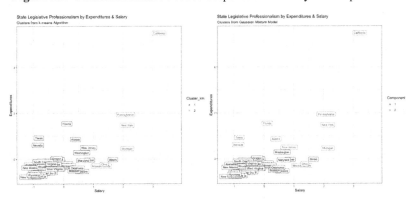

Figure 5.2 Comparing k-Means and GMM Distributions

In this figure, we can see that the original k-means algorithm on the left put far fewer states in the second (presumably "more professional") cluster, compared to the GMM approach on the right, as previously discussed. Reconciling these differences is left to the researcher. However, the important point in this exercise is to note that different clustering approaches will reveal different patterns. Thus it is good to (1) fit multiple iterations across multiple clustering techniques, and (2) to focus on overlapping results across multiple specifications. For example, though the results in Figure 5.2 differ in assignment to the second cluster, the original six states from the k-means and hierarchical approaches (minus Illinois from the hierarchical algorithm) were consistent across all clustering stages, iterations, and models. Therefore, as a conservative conclusion, it would be reasonable to suggest that these six consistent states – California, New York, Michigan, Ohio, Massachusetts, and Pennsylvania – are likely all most similar in terms of professionalism levels, at least compared to the other states.

Further, we can inspect component assignments by directly inspecting the probabilities, and then via a bar plot. To do so, we start with creating a new object, component_probs, which stores the probabilities, and then creates a new Component feature, with dichotomous assignment for probabilities greater than 0.5, as before for the plot. We then round to three decimal places and produce the output for the first 10 states in alphabetical order in Table 5.1.

```
component_probs <- as.data.frame(cbind(gmm1$x, gmm1$
                        posterior)) %>%
            mutate(Component = as.factor(ifelse(comp.1
            > 0.5, 1, 2)))

probs <- round(head(component_probs, 10), 3)
rownames(probs) <- head(states, 10)
```

In Table 5.1, most notably, we have a clearer sense of the degrees of assignment to components, where no states were barely assigned to one or the other

Table 5.1 Posterior Component Probabilities

State	p(Component 1)	p(Component 2)	Component
Alabama	0.996	0.004	1
Alaska	0.000	1.000	2
Arizona	0.000	1.000	2
Arkansas	0.992	0.008	1
California	0.000	1.000	2
Colorado	0.962	0.038	1
Connecticut	0.970	0.030	1
Delaware	0.996	0.004	1
Florida	0.000	1.000	2
Georgia	0.998	0.002	1

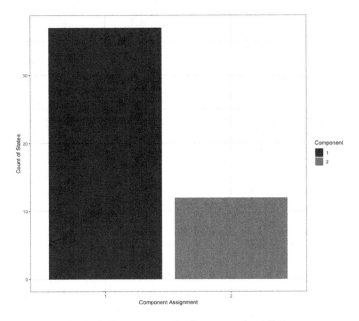

Figure 5.3 Component Assignments for All States

component (e.g., $p \approx 0.5$). This puts meat on the bones of assignment of observations to clusters/components, rather than a strict partition of an observation in one or the other cluster. Further, we can also see that the probabilities associated with assignment are quite clear, where each observation has a high probability (> 0.962) associated with one component and a relatively low probability $(1 - p)$ associated with the other component. This suggests that the observations were clearly partitioned into two groups. We can see the full assignments based on posterior probabilities in a bar chart in Figure 5.3, upon running the following code.

```
ggplot(component_probs, aes(factor(Component))) +
        geom_bar(aes(fill = Component), stat ="count") +
        labs(x = "Component Assignment",
                y = "Count of States",
                color = "Component") +
        theme_bw()
```

5.3 Internal Algorithmic Validation

Finally, we conclude this section as we have the previous two, by internally validating the performance of the GMM approach using the three validation metrics (connectivity, Dunn Index, and average silhouette width) across numerous iterations for different values of k, from two to 10. Further, as with previous approaches, we will compare the GMM approach to both k-means and hierarchical cluster approaches. Recall, we are looking for minimal values of connectivity, and maximal values of the Dunn Index scores and the average silhouette widths. Running the following code, adding "model" to the list of algorithms to test, produces the results in Table 5.2.

```
st_prof.internal.gmm<- clValid(st_scale_dist_m, 2:10,
        clMethods = c("hierarchical", "kmeans", "model"),
        validation = "internal")
summary(st_prof.internal.gmm)

par(mfrow = c(2, 2))
plot(st_prof.internal.gmm, legend = FALSE,
        type = "l",
        main = "")
```

In Table 5.2 we see that, here again, the hierarchical clustering algorithm outperformed both k-means and GMM. Further, we also see that two clusters most accurately characterize these data. Notably, here again, the hierarchical clustering algorithm with two clusters minimizes the connectivity and maximizes the Dunn Index values and the average silhouette widths compared to the other clustering techniques as well as to all other possible clusters, from three to 10.

And finally, as before, we can visualize these validation comparisons by running the following code, which results in the plot in Figure 5.4.

The new dotted line is added to the three validation plots and shows that, narrowly, the hierarchical clustering algorithm outperforms the other two approaches and the optimal number of clusters is again two.

5.4 Suggestions for Further Reading

- Figueiredo and Jain (2002)
- Moon (1996)
- Muthén and Shedden (1999)

6 Advanced Methods

In this final substantive section, I build on the logic of clustering presented throughout (both pairwise and partitioning approaches) and survey several advanced clustering techniques. Importantly, these build directly on the intuition behind clustering that we have discussed so far, where even these advanced methods are ultimately aiming to uncover the nonrandom, underlying structure that (now) likely exists in the multivariate state legislative professionalism feature space. As such, we will continue to build from our process thus

Table 5.2 Internal Validation Scores: Hierarchical vs. k-Means vs. GMM

						Number of Clusters			
	2	3	4	5	6	7	8	9	10
Internal Index: Hierarchical									
Connectivity	4.98	7.12	12.18	14.18	21.73	22.26	24.51	31.75	33.95
Dunn Index	0.52	0.52	0.48	0.48	0.36	0.36	0.36	0.20	0.20
Silhouette Width	0.77	0.72	0.59	0.58	0.39	0.32	0.31	0.29	0.28
Internal Index: k-means									
Connectivity	6.82	11.64	13.78	15.78	28.59	31.58	34.29	36.54	40.29
Dunn Index	0.20	0.20	0.37	0.37	0.14	0.14	0.16	0.16	0.18
Silhouette Width	0.75	0.58	0.57	0.55	0.32	0.32	0.33	0.32	0.34
Internal Index: GMM									
Connectivity	7.67	11.64	23.60	26.59	30.93	35.86	43.78	43.42	46.88
Dunn Index	0.11	0.20	0.08	0.14	0.11	0.11	0.08	0.12	0.12
Silhouette Width	0.66	0.58	0.35	0.34	0.33	0.30	0.32	0.34	0.31

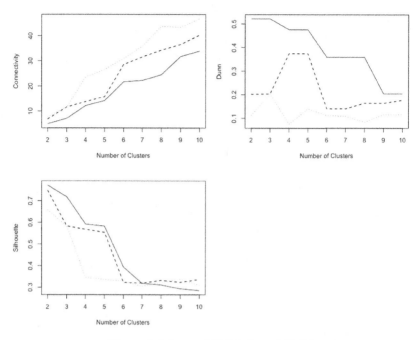

Figure 5.4 Internal Validation of GMM

far, such as assessing clusterability, as well as the introduction of our distance measures for those advanced methods that employ distance calculations.

Though there are many clustering extensions and advanced algorithms, we will briefly, and at a high level, cover fuzzy C-means clustering, density-based clustering, and partitioning around medoids clustering. Importantly, the introduction of these advanced methods is merely to pique the interest of readers. We will necessarily only scratch the surface. The goal is for readers who want to extend their understanding of clustering to look more into these and other methods that best suit their unique research needs. A second-order benefit of this brief survey of advanced methods is to demonstrate how far the field of unsupervised clustering has come, and how it continues to expand. There are state-of-the-art methods that are being developed each year. Thus, rather than frustrate readers by failing to go into great depth, I hope to inspire readers to continue to probe deeper into the exciting, rapidly developing world of cluster analysis.

6.1 Fuzzy C-means

For the first advanced method, we will continue with the soft partitioning approach and introduce fuzzy C-means (FCM) clustering. This approach to clustering allows observations to belong to multiple clusters based on similarity. Similar to GMM and unlike hard partitioning k-means clustering, FCM allows for observations to be assigned to clusters in a fractional fashion. Though similar to GMM, a key distinction between GMM and FCM is that GMM derive cluster probabilities, as GMM is a model-based clustering approach. Probabilities of cluster assignments are calculated for all observations, across all possible clusters. On the other hand, FCM is concerned with *multiple* cluster assignment based on multiple distances calculated between multiple cluster centroids. In the FCM world, we talk about membership in terms of "degrees" rather than "probabilities." This is called "fuzzy" partitioning, hence the name. For example, a data point may have fuzzy membership values of $[0.65, 0.35] \in C_1, C_2$, respectively. This data point, then, would be *assigned to both clusters*, but to differing degrees. This is the same principle as in the GMM approach, but assignment in FCM is non–model based and is thus nonparametric, preventing the (need for) calculation of probabilities. In FCM, we are interested in calculating fractional membership values, which are still distances between points and cluster centroids in feature space as in k-means, but across many clusters rather than a single cluster. The result is membership of each data point to every cluster, but to varying degrees.

We can implement FCM in R with a relatively small amount of code. The major difference in fitting an FCM algorithm compared to k-means is the specification of m, which controls the degree of fuzziness, which is the membership threshold. The m value determines the degree of conjoined membership. So, for example, in a two-dimensional case, the Y axis represents the value of m. Along the X axis, we have the spread of data points, which determines membership once above or below some threshold. For readers familiar with regression discontinuity design in causal inference, this is a similar principle, where positions above or below some cutpoint determines the class of the observation. In fitting an FCM algorithm in R, then, we must specify the fuzziness value, which should be dictated by domain expertise, as with all of the methods. But as a starting place, given the exploratory nature of clustering, setting $m = 2$ is a safe option, as this is the default value for the cmeans() function in the e1071 package, which we will be using to fit the FCM algorithm. Start with the following code.

```
# load library
library(e1071)

# fit FCM
cm <- cmeans(st_scale,
        centers = 2,
        m = 2)
```

In the code above, we can see familiar arguments in the cmeans() function (e.g., the centers argument is the same meaning as in the kmeans() function, which is the pre-specified number of clusters to govern the search). Further, note that we only input the standardized/scaled data object, and not a dissimilarity distance matrix object. This is because, by default, the cmeans() function assumes and calculates Euclidean distances between all points as the measure of spatial similarity. To change the distance metric, simply change the dist argument to be "manhattan," which is the only other distance option allowed in the cmeans() function. These arguments are detailed in the package documentation. Recall, that if a different distance metric is desired, readers can simply create their own distance object via the dist() function in base R. A cmeans object contains similar output as a kmeans object. Readers should inspect the object using the str() function in base R. For our high-level purpose, we will jump straight to a visual depiction of the clustering output from the FCM algorithm by running the following code.

```
# store a few things for plotting
st_scale$Cluster <- cm$cluster # save clusters in df
st_scale$Cluster <- as.factor( # as.factor for plotting
        ifelse(st_scale$Cluster == 1, 2, 1)
) # recode for consistency

table(st_scale$Cluster) # inspect

# FCM over expend and sal
ggplot(st_scale, aes(salary_real, expend,
                color = Cluster,
                label = states)) +
        geom_jitter() +
        geom_label(aes(label = states,
                color = Cluster),
                size = 3) +
        xlim(-1.3, 3.7) +
        labs(x = "Salary",
                y = "Expenditures",
title = "State Legislative Professionalism by Expenditures &
        Salary",
subtitle = "Clusters from Fuzzy C-Means Algorithm") +
        theme_bw()
```

In the chunk above, as with the k-means plot, we start by storing the cluster assignments from the FCM fit object. We transform this feature vector to a factor variable for plotting, and recode for consistency (e.g., cluster 1 being for the bulk of states and cluster 2 for the few states) and as the actual value assignment in cmeans is arbitrary. We then run the ggplot code to produce the output in Figure 6.1, plotted over the salary and expenditures raw values for all states.

State Legislative Professionalism by Expenditures & Salary
Clusters from Fuzzy C-Means Algorithm

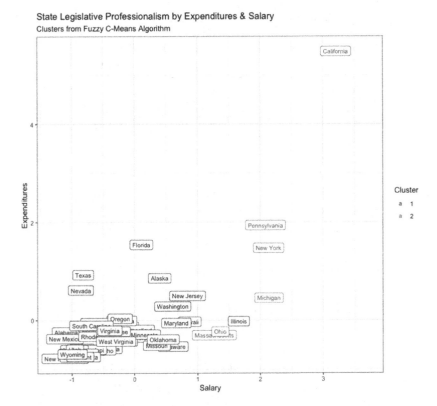

Figure 6.1 Fuzzy C-means Algorithm Fit

In Figure 6.1 we see a virtually identical configuration as with the k-means model fit. Notably, we have the same six states clustered together in blue and the remaining states clustered together in red.

However, while it seems like the two algorithms are identical, recall that, like GMM, FCM algorithms allow for fractional assignment to multiple clusters rather than hard partitioning to a single cluster. Functionally, the results in membership values greater than 0.5 are assigned to cluster 2 for plotting purposes. But, consider the multiple assignments seen most clearly in table form. Run the following chunk to get the output in Table 6.1 of the membership values for the first 10 states alphabetically.

```
states <- st$state
membership <- as.data.frame(cm$membership[1:10,])
rownames(membership) <- states[1:10]
membership <- membership[ ,c(2,1)]
colnames(membership) <- c("Cluster 1", "Cluster 2")
```

Table 6.1 Fuzzy C-means Fractional Cluster
Assignments

State	Cluster 1	Cluster 2
Alabama	0.97	0.03
Alaska	0.86	0.14
Arizona	0.57	0.43
Arkansas	0.98	0.02
California	0.26	0.74
Colorado	0.74	0.26
Connecticut	0.96	0.04
Delaware	0.94	0.06
Florida	0.82	0.18
Georgia	0.98	0.02

Note that different from the k-means hard assignment (C_k or not) and different from the large probabilities from the GMM fit, Table 6.1 demonstrates that the FCM algorithm, clearly assigning states to all clusters, has a membership less stark than the previous clustering approaches. For example, California, which has a membership assignment value to cluster 2 of 0.74 from the FCM algorithm, had a 1.0 probability of assignment to cluster 2 in the GMM approach. Further, Arizona had membership values of $[0.57, 0.43]$ for clusters 1 and 2 respectively, suggesting it is more in the middle of professional and nonprofessional legislatures. The difference and variation in cluster assignments across these approaches is notable.

The previous point underscores the utility of the FCM approach, which is that it may more accurately mirror the real world, where, for example, in assessing state legislative professionalism, hard assignment of a state as either professional or not likely makes less sense than a continuous scale of professionalism captured by multiple cluster memberships. The FCM approach is flexible enough to capture this potential.

6.2 Density-Based Clustering: DBSCAN

The next advanced method is in the density-based class of clustering. The most common algorithm in this family is called the DBSCAN algorithm, which stands for Density-Based Spatial Clustering and Application with Noise. The DBSCAN algorithm is most useful for partitioning data into less neatly defined, nonconvex clusters. As with k-means or GMM to a degree, the algorithms were focused on creating clusters in feature space that were tightly compact and spherical. Yet, often data are not distributed so cleanly. As the name suggests, then, the algorithm clusters data based on densities of observations, while handling noise in an efficient way. The handling of noise is a unique feature of this clustering approach, in that not all observations or data points must belong to a cluster, as with all other clustering approaches to this point. Rather, the DBSCAN algorithm creates optimal clusters based on point densities and spatial distances (as before), but treats distant points as outliers, and thus avoids broadening the cluster to incorporate them. The result is often unique-shaped clusters, as demonstrated in Ester et al. (1996), who invented the algorithm.

In brief, the DBSCAN algorithm is very similar to k-nearest neighbors (kNN), where the goal is to search for neighborhoods with high densities. The radius, ϵ, is the size of the neighborhoods and is preset by the researcher, along with the value of k, which is the number of points to be considered in a neighborhood. Clusters are formed based on reachability, which is the ability for some point to reach a core point, around which some neighborhood is formed. So we are still concerned with calculating distances, but the clusters include only points that are sufficiently reachable within a specified neighborhood. The idea is that in some feature space there will be a blend of natural clusters, but also noise surrounding those clusters. Parsing the clusters from the noise, all based on density, is the ultimate goal of the algorithm.

In our case with the state legislative professionalism data, several trends were interesting, suggesting these data may be well suited for the DBSCAN algorithm. For example, California was consistently an outlier, being distant from the other states along most input features. Similarly, New York seemed like an outlier as well, but primarily along the session length inputs. Further, the GMM and FCM results showed a nesting of clusters 1 and 2, more so than hierarchical clustering or k-means, where states like Arizona and Alaska were situated closer to the broader cloud of data points, but still clustered with the seemingly more professional states, like California, New York, and Pennsylvania. In sum, the results to this point suggest that the DBSCAN algorithm could provide useful nuanced clustering to more accurately configure clusters.

To implement the DBSCAN algorithm in R, we will rely on the dbscan package, though readers can fit this algorithm with other widely used packages, such as fpc. Before fitting the algorithm, we need to first create a matrix of our standardized data, and then determine the optimal neighborhood size (epsilon value, ϵ) and the minimum number of points to be considered in the neighborhood (k). In the following code chunk, we start by munging the data a bit, first redefining our state legislative professionalism object, followed by scaling the data, renaming the input features for plotting later on, and then transforming the standardized data to be an $N \times N$ matrix. With the data in proper form, we then plot the kNN distances with our minimum points specified as k. Note that there is no rule of thumb for selecting the number of minimum points. Thus, as a starting place, I specified 4 minimum points, in line with the dbscan package author's recommendation. Readers are encouraged to try multiple values of minimum points and observe whether and how the output shifts as a result. But ultimately, specifying the minimum points is crucial to determining the optimal value of ϵ, which is the neighborhood size. The conventional wisdom is to select the ϵ value at the "elbow" in a kNN distance plot. Thus, to generate the kNN distance plot, we will use the kNNdistplot() function. Upon generating the plot to ease interpretation, I overlaid a red line at this point, which is ≈ 1.2, via the abline() function in base R.

```
# load the dbscan library
library(dbscan)

# redefine scaled df and munge
st <- x %>%
        filter(sessid == "2009/10") %>%
        select(-c(fips, stateabv, sessid, mds1, mds2, year)) %>%
        na.omit(st); skim(st)

st_scale <- data.frame(scale(st[,2:5])) %>%
        rename(`Total Length` = t_slength,
               `Regular Length` = slength,
               `Salary` = salary_real,
               `Expenditures` = expend) %>%
        as.matrix()

# determine optimal epsilon value
kNNdistplot(st_scale,
            k = 4)
abline(h = 1.2,
       col = "red")
```

The code produces the plot in Figure 6.2, showing that indeed the value at the elbow in the plotted 4-NN distance is ≈ 1.2, suggesting 1.2 is the optimal neighborhood size to govern the algorithm fit.[6]

To fit the DBSCAN algorithm, we need to first supply the standardized data matrix of our four input features, followed by specifying the neighborhood size, which is the eps argument. Per the results in Figure 6.2, we set this value at 1.2. Then, the final required argument is minPts, which sets the minimum number of points to be considered in the neighborhood. *Note*: this value should be the same as the k value previously supplied in the kNNdistplot() function to get

---

[6] As with setting the minimum number of points discussion above, readers are encouraged to change the ϵ value and observe how the resultant cluster configuration changes as a result. The potential for variability underscores the need for researchers to be open about their process and present all output for all specifications tested.

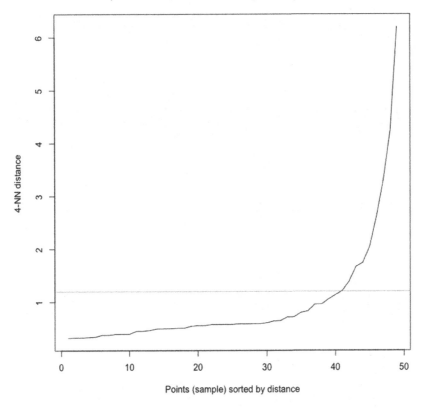

Figure 6.2 Determining the Optimal Value of ϵ

the optimal ϵ value. The next bit of code is the visual result of the DBSCAN algorithm as a lattice plot across all raw values of our input feature vectors. We specified the color based on the cluster configuration, where red points are the cluster(s), and blue points are the "outliers." Running the following chunk produces the plot in Figure 6.3 across all input features. This plot is followed by the full assignment solution in Figure 6.4, which is produced using the preceding chunk of code.

```
# run the algorithm
dbscan_fit <- dbscan(st_scale,
eps = 1.2,
minPts = 4)

# visualize across all raw values
pairs(st_scale,
      col = ifelse(dbscan_fit$cluster == 1,
           "#F8766D", "#00BFC4"),
      pch = 19)
```

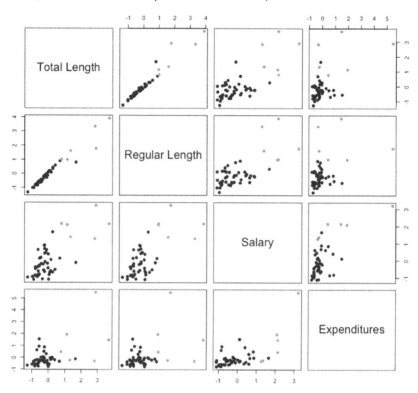

Figure 6.3 DBSCAN Algorithm Fit across All Input Features

```
# cluster assignment
rownames(st_scale) <- st$state

fviz_cluster(dbscan_fit, st_scale,
        repel = TRUE,
        show.clust.cent = FALSE,
        outlier.color = "#00BFC4",
        labelsize = 7,
        pointsize = 1.5,
        main = "Cluster Assignments from DBSCAN
                Algorithm") +
theme_bw()
```

Strikingly, the algorithm returned only a single cluster of red points, and six states were considered as outliers. But interestingly, we know from the previous clustering results that these six points are the same six states that were previously considered as more "professional." Regardless of assumed professionalism, though, these results strongly support the notion that there is something distinct about these six states, when considered alongside all previous findings from the clustering algorithms. Even though the DBSCAN

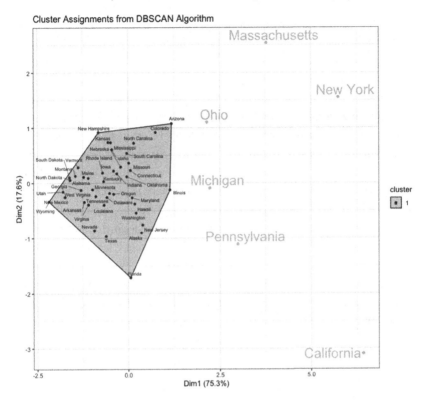

Figure 6.4 DBSCAN Algorithm Fit

algorithm treats these states as outliers, as they are the same as the other states in previous results, we can reasonably conclude that these six states could be considered a less dense cluster in their own right. But the high-density cluster found by the DBSCAN algorithm is the remaining states in red.

6.3 Partitioning around Medoids: PAM

Finally, we turn to a method much more similar to k-means than the previous two advanced methods: partitioning around medoids, or the "PAM" algorithm. This approach is often referred to as "k-medoids," giving a nod to the similarity with k-means. The idea of k-medoids is quite simple in light of our coverage of k-means. The algorithm is also a hard partitioning method that creates clusters based on minimizing the intracluster distances between a centroid and the cluster members. The key difference between k-means, though, is that the cluster centroid is an actual data point rather than a computed cluster mean. Other than this point of deviation, the algorithms are the same.

The PAM algorithm is by far the most commonly used k-medoids algorithm, as it is best suited for small to medium-sized data sets, as are most of those encountered in social and political research. Yet, for big data applications, the CLARA algorithm is more appropriate, as seen in its full name, which is Clustering Large Applications. As our data is rather small, we will focus on implementing the PAM algorithm.

As we have already standardized our data, we are ready to fit the PAM algorithm using the pam() function from the cluster package. The arguments are similar to fitting a k-means algorithm. We input the rescaled data object and specify the number of clusters we want to search for by passing some value (2 in our case) to the k argument. A difference between PAM and k-means in R, though, is that we need to specify a distance metric, which will be Euclidean distance for consistency. *Note:* if this argument is left blank, the algorithm assumes a distance matrix is the input data object (i.e., using the dist() function in base R to create a distance matrix object). Readers are encouraged to inspect the package documentation for further details on fitting the algorithm.

```
# fit the algorithm
pam_fit <- pam(st_scale,
               k = 2,
               metric = "euclidean")
```

Running the previous chunk of code results in the output in Figure 6.5. Here, the results are nearly identical, with the difference being the inclusion of Illinois in the second cluster, resulting in seven states being clustered in cluster 2, with the remaining states in cluster 1 as before. This was the same pattern we saw in the hierarchical clustering (with Ward's linkage) application at the outset, with seven states instead of six in the k-means and GMM applications.

As mentioned, the PAM algorithm is quite similar to k-means, with the exception of specifying the cluster centroid, which in the case of PAM is an actual data point rather than some computed cluster mean as in k-means. Thus, and in light of the inclusion of Illinois in the PAM output above in Figure 6.5, let's directly compare the PAM and k-means output side by side in Figure 6.6 for a closer look.

Here we can see that, indeed, the only difference between these two algorithms is the inclusion of Illinois in cluster 2 in PAM, compared to its exclusion in the k-means approach. This point reiterates that multiple specifications and iterations are valuable when approaching clustering for political and social science research questions. Note that at this point you could (should) check the internal validation of the PAM algorithm compared to the other clustering

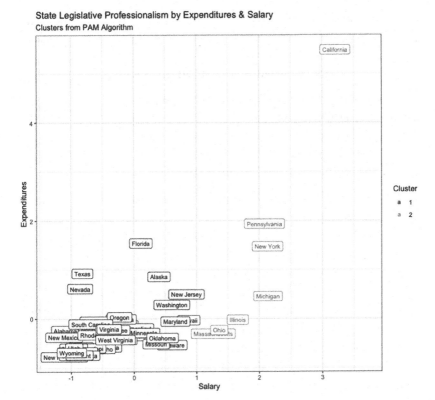

Figure 6.5 PAM Algorithm Fit

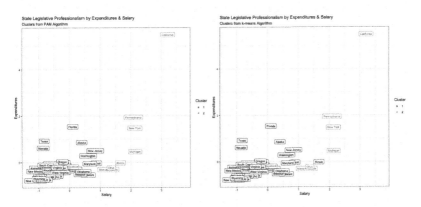

Figure 6.6 Comparing the PAM and K-means Algorithms

algorithms specified to this point by simply including "pam" in the `clMethods` argument in the `clValid()` function as demonstrated earlier in this Element.

6.4 Suggestions for Further Reading

- Bezdek, Ehrlich, and Full (1984) (Fuzzy C-means)
- Ester et al. (1996) (DBSCAN)
- Kaufman and Rousseeuw (2009) (PAM/k-medoids)

7 Conclusion

This element has offered an introduction of some of the most prominent approaches to clustering and classifying data, using data on state legislative professionalism. With four raw input features consisting of total session length, regular session length, legislator salaries and expenditures per legislator, we were able to both introduce and demonstrate application of the most common clustering approaches: hierarchical, k-means clustering (hard partitioning), and model-based Gaussian mixture models using the expectation-maximization algorithm (soft partitioning). Building on these foundation approaches, as well as the mechanics of setting the stage for clustering applications (e.g., assessing clusterability, calculating distance), we concluded the substantive sections with a high-level tour of more-advanced, state-of-the-art clustering techniques: fuzzy C-means clustering, density-based cluster using the DBSCAN algorithm, and k-medoids clustering using the PAM algorithm. In addition to many chunks of R code and the use of real data, readers have been introduced to the process of approaching a real question in social and political research, and then the steps to implement the most common form of unsupervised machine learning to help make sense of the data: clustering.

7.1 Some Trade-offs in Method Selection

It is important to remember that when approaching an unlabeled and often messy data set about which little is known, different clustering methods as well as internal choices within each (e.g., linkage method specification) will influence the resultant patterns and cluster configurations. This is an inherent difficulty associated with unsupervised machine learning. To safeguard against this ambiguity, it was recommended throughout this Element that researchers do two things, at a minimum: first, check the internal validation of each algorithm across multiple specifications (e.g., altering the value of clusters, k, to search for); and second, fit multiple clustering algorithms and compare the configurations to each other in an effort to reveal consistencies (and thus the likely "true," natural clustering patterns that exist) as well as inconsistencies (and thus likely "random" aberrations in the data, or unique patterns as a function of a single clustering technique).

As a result, researchers should be aware of the trade-offs that exist when selecting a given clustering technique or set of techniques to address some question of interest. Though mentioned at various stages throughout this Element, some of these trade-offs bear repeating.

- No single clustering approach or algorithm is inherently *right*; each approach differs in important ways, and differences should be carefully appreciated and taken into consideration during the modeling phase of a research program
- Remember that differences exist in broad clustering approaches: hierarchical (pairwise clustering) versus partitioning or subdividing the data into groups
- Within partitioning, there is hard partitioning, which is strict assignment of observations to a single, nonoverlapping cluster; and there is also soft partitioning, which is either probabilistically assigning observations to several possible clusters (e.g., Gaussian mixture models) or allowing observations to partially exist in multiple clusters (e.g., fuzzy C-means clustering)
- Neat, well-defined, and compact clusters are not always possible in the real world; thus, advanced techniques like the DBSCAN algorithm may be more appropriate, as they search for density-based clusters in a sea of noise, thus allowing some observations to belong to clusters, and treating others as outliers
- All algorithms and approaches differ mostly in how they define and measure unique quantities. For example, regarding k-means and k-medoids, the former computes a cluster mean and calculates distances between observations and that centroid to minimize the cost function, which is usually the intracluster sum of squared deviations; the latter simply selects an actual observation to act as the cluster centroid, and proceeds to optimize the cluster configuration the same way as k-means

References

Anscombe, F. J. 1973. "Graphs in statistical analysis." *The American Statistician* 27:17–21.

Baumer, Benjamin S., Daniel T. Kaplan, and Nicholas J. Horton. 2017. *Modern Data Science with R.* Chapman and Hall/CRC.

Benaglia, Tatiana, Didier Chauveau, David Hunter, and Derek Young. 2009. "mixtools: An R package for analyzing finite mixture models." *Journal of Statistical Software* 32(6):1–29.

Bezdek, James C., and Richard J. Hathaway. 2002. VAT: A tool for visual assessment of (cluster) tendency. In *IJCNN'02. Proceedings of the 2002 International Joint Conference on Neural Networks.* Vol. 3 IEEE pp. 2225–2230.

Bezdek, James C., Robert Ehrlich, and William Full. 1984. "FCM: The Fuzzy C-Means clustering algorithm." *Computers & Geosciences* 10(2–3):191–203.

Bouveyron, Charles, Gilles Celeux, T. Brendan Murphy, and Adrian E. Raftery. 2019. *Model-Based Clustering and Classification for Data Science: With Applications in R.* Cambridge University Press.

Bowen, Daniel C., and Zachary Greene. 2014. "Should we measure professionalism with an index? A note on theory and practice in state legislative professionalism research." *State Politics & Policy Quarterly* 14(3): 277–296.

Brock, Guy, Vasyl Pihur, Susmita Datta, Somnath Datta, et al. 2011. "clValid, an R package for cluster validation." *Journal of Statistical Software.*

Day, William H. E., and Herbert Edelsbrunner. 1984. "Efficient algorithms for agglomerative hierarchical clustering methods." *Journal of Classification* 1(1):7–24.

Ester, Martin, Hans-Peter Kriegel, Jörg Sander, Xiaowei Xu, et al. 1996. A density-based algorithm for discovering clusters in large spatial databases with noise. In *Kdd.* Vol. 96 pp. 226–231.

Figueiredo, Mario A. T., and Anil K. Jain. 2002. "Unsupervised learning of finite mixture models." *IEEE Transactions on Pattern Analysis and Machine Intelligence* 24(3):381–396.

Friedman, Jerome, Trevor Hastie, and Robert Tibshirani. 2001. *The Elements of Statistical Learning.* Springer series in statistics. New York, NY.

Gong, Xiaoliang, Bozhong Long, Kun Fang, Zongling Di, Yichu Hou, and Lei Cao. 2016. A prediction based on clustering and personality questionnaire data for IGD risk: A preliminary work. In *2016 12th International Conference on Natural Computation, Fuzzy Systems and Knowledge Discovery (ICNC-FSKD).* IEEE pp. 1699–1703.

Hara, Kotaro, Abigail Adams, Kristy Milland, Saiph Savage, Chris Callison-Burch, and Jeffrey P. Bigham. 2018. A data-driven analysis of workers' earnings on Amazon Mechanical Turk. In *Proceedings of the 2018 CHI Conference on Human Factors in Computing Systems.* ACM p. 449.

Hartigan, John A., and Manchek A. Wong. 1979. "Algorithm AS 136: A k-means clustering algorithm." *Journal of the Royal Statistical Society. Series C (Applied Statistics)* 28(1):100–108.

Johnson, Stephen C. 1967. "Hierarchical clustering schemes." *Psychometrika* 32(3):241–254.

Kanungo, Tapas, David M. Mount, Nathan S. Netanyahu, Christine D. Piatko, Ruth Silverman, and Angela Y. Wu. 2002. "An efficient k-means clustering algorithm: Analysis and implementation." *IEEE Transactions on Pattern Analysis & Machine Intelligence* (7):881–892.

Kassambara, Alboukadel. 2017. *Practical Guide to Cluster Analysis in R: Unsupervised Machine Learning.* Vol. 1 STHDA.

Kaufman, Leonard, and Peter J. Rousseeuw. 2009. *Finding Groups in Data: an Introduction to Cluster Analysis.* Vol. 344 John Wiley & Sons.

Matejka, Justin, and George Fitzmaurice. 2017. Same stats, different graphs: generating datasets with varied appearance and identical statistics through simulated annealing. In *Proceedings of the 2017 CHI Conference on Human Factors in Computing Systems.* ACM pp. 1290–1294.

Moon, Todd K. 1996. "The expectation-maximization algorithm." *IEEE Signal Processing Magazine* 13(6):47–60.

Muthén, Bengt, and Kerby Shedden. 1999. "Finite mixture modeling with mixture outcomes using the EM algorithm." *Biometrics* 55(2): 463–469.

Squire, Peverill. 1992. "Legislative professionalization and membership diversity in state legislatures." *Legislative Studies Quarterly* pp. 69–79.

Squire, Peverill. 2000. "Uncontested seats in state legislative elections." *Legislative Studies Quarterly* pp. 131–146.

Squire, Peverill. 2007. "Measuring state legislative professionalism: The squire index revisited." *State Politics & Policy Quarterly* 7(2): 211–227.

Squire, Peverill. 2017. "A Squire Index update." *State Politics & Policy Quarterly* 17(4):361–371.

Tukey, John W. 1980. "We need both exploratory and confirmatory." *The American Statistician* 34(1):23–25.

Wickham, Hadley, and Garrett Grolemund. 2016. *R for Data Science: Import, Tidy, Transform, Visualize, and Model Data.* O'Reilly Media, Inc.

Acknowledgments

I am grateful to my friends and colleagues who supported me during the writing of this manuscript both at the University of Chicago, as well as at the College of William & Mary. I am also appreciative of the graduate students who took my *Unsupervised Machine Learning* course at UChicago. They offered me ample room (and patience) to "test out" many of these examples and debug a lot of the original code.

My friend and software-colleague Fong Chun Chan is also owed sincere gratitude for his invaluable perspective on Gaussian mixture models. Also, I am so thankful for the warm and welcoming open science and R communities for many things from offering incredible packages to supporting me as I write and deploy my own. The R community specifically is owed a great amount from scholars, researchers, and data scientists across the world who reap immeasurable benefits from the ingenuity of honest and talented programmers and developers.

I also thank the series editors R. Michael Alvarez and Neal Beck for their consistent support, as well as the anonymous reviewers whose comments greatly strengthened the content. Specifically, I am deeply indebted to Neal Beck who has been immensely helpful throughout the writing and revision of this manuscript. This work would not be what it is had Neal been withholding of his kindness, expertise, and guidance.

And finally, I am forever grateful to my bride, Becky, who has tirelessly supported me throughout the writing of this manuscript, and everything else in my life. She makes all things utterly vibrant and full, and is a constant reminder that there is so much more to life than work. She is owed far more than these few words could express.

Data Availability Statement

R scripts replicating all the numerical and visual results are available at www.cambridge.org/waggoner and can be run interactively online via Code Ocean. Hyperlinks and DOI's for each section are given below.

Section 1: https://doi.org/10.24433/CO.8117355.v1
Section 2: https://doi.org/10.24433/CO.7170712.v1
Section 3: https://doi.org/10.24433/CO.5889138.v1
Section 4: https://doi.org/10.24433/CO.4366133.v1
Section 5: https://doi.org/10.24433/CO.5400292.v1
Section 6: https://doi.org/10.24433/CO.5351178.v1

Cambridge Elements $\overline{\overline{=}}$

Quantitative and Computational Methods for the Social Sciences

R. Michael Alvarez
California Institute of Technology

R. Michael Alvarez has taught at the California Institute of Technology his entire career, focusing on elections, voting behavior, election technology, and research methodologies. He has written or edited a number of books (recently, *Computational Social Science: Discovery and Prediction,* and *Evaluating Elections: A Handbook of Methods and Standards*) and numerous academic articles and reports.

Nathaniel Beck
New York University

Nathaniel Beck is Professor of Politics at NYU (and Affiliated Faculty at the NYU Center for Data Science) where he has been since 2003; before which he was Professor of Political Science at the University of California, San Diego. He is the founding editor of the quarterly, *Political Analysis.* He is a fellow of both the American Academy of Arts and Sciences and the Society for Political Methodology.

About the Series

The Elements Series *Quantitative and Computational Methods for the Social Sciences* contains short introductions and hands-on tutorials to innovative methodologies. These are often so new that they have no textbook treatment or no detailed treatment on how the method is used in practice. Among emerging areas of interest for social scientists, the series presents machine learning methods, the use of new technologies for the collection of data and new techniques for assessing causality with experimental and quasi-experimental data.

Cambridge Elements $\equiv$

Quantitative and Computational Methods for the Social Sciences

Elements in the Series

Twitter as Data
Zachary C. Steinert-Threlkeld

A Practical Introduction to Regression Discontinuity Designs: Foundations
Matias D. Cattaneo, Nicolás Idrobo and Rocío Titiunik

Agent-Based Models of Social Life: Fundamentals
Michael Laver

Agent-Based Models of Polarization and Ethnocentrism
Michael Laver

Images as Data for Social Science Research
Nora Webb Williams, Andreu Casas and John D. Wilkerson

Target Estimation and Adjustment Weighting for Survey Nonresponse and Sampling Bias
Devin Caughey, Adam J. Berinsky, Sara Chatfield, Erin Hartman, Eric Schickler and Jasjeet S. Sekhon

Text Analysis in Python for Social Scientists: Discovery and Exploration
Dirk Hovy

Unsupervised Machine Learning for Clustering in Political and Social Research
Philip D. Waggoner

A full series listing is available at: www.cambridge.org/QCMSS

Printed in the United States
By Bookmasters